Say Yes to Pears

Thank you for all your
support! Go Tigers!

Brent Putty

NCTE Editorial Board

Say Yes to Pears

Food Literacy in and beyond the English Classroom

Joseph Franzen
Cuba-Rushford High School, Cuba, New York

Brent Peters
Fern Creek High School, Louisville, Kentucky

NATIONAL COUNCIL OF TEACHERS OF ENGLISH
1111 W. KENYON ROAD, URBANA, ILLINOIS 61801-1096
WWW.NCTE.ORG

Staff Editor: Bonny Graham

Interior Design: Jenny Jensen Greenleaf

Cover Design: Pat Mayer

Cover Images: iStock.com/achtung_ein, iStock.com/RapidEye, iStock.com/marcoventuriniautieri

NCTE Stock Number: 42417; eStock Number: 42424
ISBN 978-0-8141-4241-7; eISBN 978-0-8141-4242-4

Library of Congress Cataloging-in-Publication Data

Names: Franzen, Joseph, 1983- author. | Peters, Brent, 1975- author.
Title: Say yes to pears : food literacy in and beyond the English classroom / by Joseph Franzen and Brent Peters.
Description: Urbana, Illinois : National Council of Teachers of English, [2019] | Includes bibliographical references and index.
Identifiers: LCCN 2019000314 (print) | LCCN 2019018494 (ebook) | ISBN 9780814142424 (ebook) | ISBN 9780814142417 (pbk) | ISBN 9780814142424 (ebk)
Subjects: LCSH: English language—Study and teaching (Secondary) | Food—Study and teaching (Secondary) | Food industry and trade—Study and teaching (Secondary) | Culturally relevant pedagogy.
Classification: LCC LB1631 (ebook) | LCC LB1631 .F6955 2019 (print) | DDC 428.4071/2—dc23
LC record available at https://lccn.loc.gov/2019000314

Contents

Foreword: Words from Dixie Goswami

Over the past few years, I've been in company with Joe Franzen and Brent Peters often: in Bread Loaf classrooms in Vermont, in their Fern Creek High School classrooms, at national conferences, at meetings of the Kentucky Bread Loaf Teacher Network, in their school garden, in their kitchens (and mine), and always in touch on Bread-Net and by phone. With Beverly Moss, director of the Bread Loaf Teacher Network, I joined their Cooking 101 class in 2016 when Milo Quinn read "The Guilt of Biscuits and Gravy" and enjoyed a meal prepared for us. Joe and Brent are my mentors, my friends, my colleagues. Just as *Say Yes to Pears* is evidence of what young people can do when they have learning opportunities that fit and value their experiences, Joe and Brent are evidence of what teachers can do when they're in the company of administrators like Nathan Meyer and Rebecca Nichols and colleagues who share the belief that youth have the potential to be a force for progress and positive social change in their families, communities, and the world. The web of *Say Yes to Pears* connections includes Bread Loaf courses and the Bread Loaf Teacher Network, which supports collaboration and shared inquiry and honors the stories and theories of its members: www.middlebury.blse/bltnmag.

Say Yes to Pears is located within the growing body of work in youth studies and youth engagement that points to the significance of young people in contributing to public discourse around issues of concern to their everyday lives, including their education, arguing that young people be given a more significant voice that reaches public audiences, local and beyond. While *Say Yes to Pears* is in the tradition of Shirley Brice Heath's *Ways with Words* and *Words at Work and Play;* Barbara Cervone's What Kids Can Do organization; Jacqueline Jones Royster's scholarship, including the keynote address "Literacy and

Civic Engagement"; Valerie Kinloch's *Harlem on Our Minds*; Ken Macorie's *The I-Search Paper*; Nancie Atwell's *In the Middle,* 2nd edition; and David Kirkland's *A Search Past Silence: The Literacy of Young Black Men, Say Yes to Pears* presents a powerful, multivoiced narrative about academic, social, and civic engagement, a well-documented story of multidisciplinary teaching and learning that contrasts sharply with commercialized, routinized curricula. This book represents a new and inclusive genre for and by teachers and young people, intended for diverse public audiences as well as educators. *Say Yes to Pears* is revolutionary in that it brings together student writings alongside those of experienced teacher-scholars and provides a definitive statement about the potential of youth participatory education.

I recommend reading *Say Yes to Pears* several times, first for the pleasure that comes from the compelling narratives and images that bring Joe, Brent, and the students alive. Then read to discover the strategies and structures that empower teachers and students—starting with a handshake. Finally, read to consider the different perspectives and analyses that emerge and to bring your own to the table.

Here's a passage that gives me plenty to think about. Isn't that what a book should do?

> I'm still just a student. I have no degree in English. I've never edited anything that was meant to be published besides a high school literary magazine. I'm just a kid that got the first shot at editing a book meant to teach teachers. Editing the book was a ton of fun and opened my eyes to a potential career path. . . . It was an odd experience. Mr. Franzen and Mr. Peters treated me as an equal as we all edited the document: this was especially visible as the final changes were being made. . . . [M]y ideas or critiques were not disregarded just because I was a student. That's a rare experience, even in classes where the teachers try to treat their students like adults; how many would trust a student to edit and format a section of anything they planned to publish, let alone an entire chapter? The class hasn't just taught me about editing either; no, I learned a very important lesson about long-term group work. You don't necessarily have to like each other to get all the work done. . . . [This class] forced us to work together and be problem solvers. It allowed me to learn about myself without sacrificing the other education.

Isn't that what a class should do?

Dixie Goswami, Professor Emerita, Clemson University
Special Projects Director, Bread Loaf Teacher Network
Director, Write to Change Foundation

Introduction: Meet the Authors

Tattoos and Homebrew (Joe Franzen)

A young woman, two AR-15s crossed over the image of a globe underwritten by the words "Save the World" tattooed on her shoulder, was the first person to let me know about Brent Peters. With the bustling atmosphere of the farmers market in the background, throwing frozen chicken body parts into a cotton bag for a customer, she said he was a friend and would be teaching at Fern Creek High School (FCHS)—where I had just accepted a job—starting in the fall. FCHS was known at the time for having lockdowns and being audited by the state for low test scores. I'm not sure what it was about the situation, but my anxiety level shot sky high, and I decided to steer clear of this Brent Peters fellow, who most likely had a tattoo across his chest of a flaming skull surrounded by the words "Teach or Die!" Luckily, I didn't stick with that decision.

At that point in my life, I had been in Louisville, Kentucky, for four years and teaching at Shelby West Middle School, about thirty miles to the east. In spite of coming from a family of educators, I denied the calling until my final semester at Washington and Lee University (W&L), when the teacher recruitment program Teach Kentucky extended the welcome to come west. With my truck packed and classes at the University of Louisville for an MAT starting the next morning, I left W&L the day after graduation to start the next stage of my life—as an educator.

The first year was a trial by fire: first teaching job, no classroom experience, sets of thirty twelve-year-olds who couldn't sit still and needed to be convinced that someone long dead and decomposed held a secret to improving their lives. During my four years at West Middle, I reached into my past to engage my students in the study of history. I used the storytelling of my Philadelphia-bred German family to connect myself to my past and to help students connect to their own. I used my upbringing in the garden, with ducks, and on the farm to connect students to the ancient acts of planting—building a garden, getting dirty, and tapping into the emotions of a farmer waiting patiently for a seed to sprout—and to the success of reaping what you sow. I used my knowledge from growing up in the kitchen to engage student bodies in the movements and techniques of the past, such as feeling the texture of elongating protein strands while kneading bread, smelling the pungent aroma of fermenting cabbage in a crock, and identifying when something is "done" without using a timer. Fostered by the Mennonite church and the experience of growing up in a blended family, I used my intense understanding of the power of a shared meal to bring students from all backgrounds together in a common perspective through which to engage the past as active participants. In reality, this looked like a ragged garden made with old tires; sporadic interdisciplinary, hands-on, food-based lessons in a world history class; and, in place of a study hall, a food-based class that explored identity, food systems, and how we engage with the world. This last piece was the only part of the day when I didn't feel like I was putting on a show. It was the part of the day when we all laughed, learned, and seamlessly shared the job of teaching and learning with the thirty sixth- and seventh-grade students who had chosen to participate in the endeavor. I knew this was what I wanted to do and what students needed to experience.

While bottling some home brew with my colleague Paul Barnwell, Houston Barber, a principal from the neighboring school district of Jefferson County, came over to Paul's house in an effort to recruit my friend. Principal Barber made Fern Creek High School sound like the most amazing environment for an educator despite being labeled a "failing school" by the state, having half of its teachers removed, and expecting massive oversight by the powers that be. Paul was sold, and I invited Dr. Barber over to my Germantown urban homestead for omelets the following weekend to discuss a possible way to continue what I had started in West Middle. He came; we collected eggs from my chickens in the backyard, harvested sweet peppers from my front yard, and made some delicious omelets in the kitchen. As we sat on the porch discussing the positive impacts of my food class on identity, community, and critical thinking, Dr. Barber turned to me and invited me to teach at Fern Creek. When I asked what I would teach, he looked at the omelet and the garden and said, "All of it."

So I ended up at Fern Creek High School, a high-poverty, "failing" high school where the students were much larger and more intimidating than my seventh graders, with the mandate to help rebuild school community. It seemed like the perfect time to take the advice of my farmers market chicken-throwing friend and connect with Brent Peters. He does not have flaming skulls tattooed on his body, and, over the course of five years, he pushed my ability as an educator to new levels as we created a community of learners, explorers, thinkers, writers, and activists in a school most people thought was the dregs.

Clean Plates (Brent Peters)

My culinary wake-up call came when I was eight years old. One Saturday morning in our southern Indiana home, I smelled a mixture of French toast, pancakes, and powdered sugar. I ran down to the kitchen and saw Mom forming circles of dough with cookie cutters. She announced that Dad was out on the back porch, making donuts for breakfast. *Dad?* Dad had two solid dishes in his cooking repertoire—grilled cheese and fried bologna sandwiches, both served with Campbell's vegetable soup. He could make donuts—*at our house!*

My brother and sister, Brian and Becki, and I watched Dad place the dough gently into the FryDaddy, where the donuts bubbled in the hot oil. Dad pulled them out cautiously, then quickly placed them in a paper bag full of powdered sugar, sealed them off, and shook the bag. When he opened the bag, we beheld the powdered sugar–covered marvels—donuts and donut holes. Before this day, I had thought you could only buy donuts at a bakery. We cleaned our plates, and the memory stayed with me like the powdered sugar on my fingers.

Much later, after I graduated from Bellarmine University in Louisville, Kentucky, with a degree in English, I had an overwhelming desire to get closer to the wonder of cooking. Chef Bruce Ucán at the Mayan Gypsy (now the Mayan Café, https://themayancafe.com/) gave me a chance, even though I had little cooking experience. Chef Bruce taught me how cooking and teaching go together.

At Mayan Gypsy, I was engrossed in the sensory overload and overlap of working in a professional kitchen. I was traveling through new experiences each night, via the sounds of frying plantains and the popping of pumpkin seeds on the flat top, and through the pungent, knock-you-down smell of chilies roasting in preparation for a mole sauce.

As I watched Chef Bruce on the line, I knew that all of us in the kitchen were helping him tell his story through food—through the cochinita pibil wrapped in banana leaves and slowly roasted in achiote sauce, through the shrimp ceviche with fresh lime juice, and through the chayote relleno squashes topped with cotija cheese. I saw how a plate could combine seasonal ingredients and strong flavors with the deep emotion of memory, landscape, and home all in one. I read appreciation on the clean plates that came back to the dishwasher. As I washed those plates, I knew I wasn't the only one stamping my passport each night.

We all have powerful food stories—tied to the deepest layers of who we are. Whether that story leads to the back porch, to the Yucatán, or to some other place in our memory, food is a journey that leads to tasty and delicious wonder. When we share in stories related to food, the plates always come back clean, and we are made hungry for more. I had no idea at the time, but my work in the kitchen was preparing me to become a teacher and to think about teaching in relation to cooking. When I think of how cooking and teaching go together, I think of clean plates.

Which Part of Me Is Last Night's Dinner? (Joe Franzen)

Trying to give credit to the pedagogical theories and ideas in this book is akin to figuring out what part of your body is made from last night's dinner or from Thanksgiving the previous fall. You know you consumed it. You know it's part of you. But nailing down the exact manifestation of past consumption is an impossible challenge.

Reflected in this book are all of the informal and formal educators who have shaped us and formed our conscious and unconscious teacher personalities and styles. I can remember those teachers because I become them a little bit every day, whether it's Thomas Ruth from late-night, tea-fueled learning sessions at The Hill School, or W&L's Harvey Markowitz driving us through the desert on the Mexican border for the love of Tohono O'odham culture. At the same time, the lessons from my daughters, Eleanor and Hazel, and my wife, Elizabeth (thank you for your support in this process), have made me a more patient, compassionate, and creative teacher as I grew into the roles of "pop" and husband.

When you subscribe to the pedagogical histories of place-based and project-based learning and to the development of critical thought and questioning, these approaches become your definition of what teaching is. However, in reflecting on how I came into contact with these methods, I think about the educators, authors, and thinkers whose works can provide interested educators with a greater depth of understanding about these methods than we can provide here. Read, for example, the classic *Teaching as a Subversive Activity* by Neil Postman and Charles Weingartner, which has led myriad educators to hold high the banner of questioning what the purpose of education is and what it can be. Howard Zinn, especially in *A People's History of the United States,* allowed me to question the texts taught as dogma and to open new avenues in the classroom for questions and conversation on topics that oftentimes are treated as static.

Philosophers, gardeners, and/or naturalists Wendell Berry, Wes Jackson, Alice Waters, Bill McKibben, Michael Pollan, Tom Wessels, and Richard Louv, although not traditionally cited as pedagogical leaders in public education, helped me build a framework in which I constructed my educational world. David Sobel, specifically in *Childhood and Nature: Design Principles for Educators,* became my sage for place-based and project-based learning. David Foster Wallace was a guide to an interdisciplinary, holistic approach to the world that allowed food to connect to ethics, to connect to what it means to be a modern

American, to what it means to be human beyond the banalities of daily life . . . and to translate that for kids.

The CARDS program, a sponsored master's in education with a concentration in diversity literacy at the University of Louisville, empowered me to speak on what I thought was taboo and terrifying. Through classes focused on the modern dynamics of poverty, gender studies, pan-African studies, and the spectrum of critical theories, I found the words to talk about inequality, racism, discrimination, and sexism, and to bring those words into the high school classroom, where students yearned to talk about these topics while uncovering the ways the world works around them.

Just as I cannot remember every meal that has added structure to my body and energy to my spirit, I know I am forgetting so many authors, teachers, and lessons that formed the program and activities you will read about here. None of this is new. It's just the dish that Brent and I have made from the local ingredients, past education, and luck of finding an audience ready to dine on the menu.

The Echoes Are in the Brownie Batter (Brent Peters)

I used to bake a lot with my Grandma Trunick. One of our favorite things to make together was brownies. We used a boxed mix, but the result was never quite the same because we always changed something. Extra oil made the brownies gooey. More flour led to more cakey brownies.

Then we got inventive.

We added caramel squares to the batter. We topped the brownies with powdered sugar. We added chocolate chips, cherry preserves, and marshmallow cream. We served brownies à la mode with fudge syrup, made our own icing, and used (and sampled) the packaged icing, and then added sprinkles (chocolate and rainbow). Each time, we learned something new. I learned about learning—how learning requires permission to mess up and to experiment. I would have an idea, and my granny suggested that we test it out. The most memorable time was when Grandma Trunick looked at me and said, "You're going to be a chef."

I had never heard such genuine praise spoken directly to me. Granny's words still echo inside of me because she spoke to me with her eyes, her voice, and her heart. I did become a chef. I have learned to recognize the voice of those who speak to me with the same sincerity as my grandma. I owe this book to so many people who, through their words and actions, have influenced me and enabled me and so many others to find new ways through the world.

This book is here because of people like Dixie Goswami, Emily Bartels, Rex Lee Jim, Ceci Lewis, David Wandera, Beverly Moss, Tom McKenna, Bruce Ucán, Ivor Chodkowski, Brian and Ellen Peters, Darrell Kingery, Joe Franzen, Paul Barnwell, Beau Baker, Jai Wilson, Emily Kirkpatrick, Kurt Austin, Bonny Graham, Vickie Joyner, Jenny Aberli, Becky Peters, William and Patricia Peters, Rodney and Sherry Kosfeld, all of my family and friends, Bellarmine University and Middlebury Bread Loaf staff and professors, and students and staff at FCHS. They are all my mentors, teachers, and friends. They have encouraged me to find new paths. They also speak with their words, their eyes, and their hearts. There are so many others whom I have been able to meet and learn from who appear here too through their echoes.

Foremost, this book emerges from classes with professors at the Middlebury College Bread Loaf School of English. My clarion call was my first class, Hip-Hop as Social Justice Texts. Professor David Kirkland made the argument that hip-hop is already in the classroom—and that by not including hip-hop as a text, we were missing an opportunity to share a literacy, a space, and an opportunity with our students. Kirkland taught us to read hip-hop as a way to engage with and connect to students' lives and the world. I kept thinking how food worked the same way, and one morning while eating pancakes, I had a maple syrup eureka moment: *food is hip-hop*. Food, like hip-hop, is also already in the classroom and in our lives. We could read food, cook food, and share food as a powerful way of connecting us to the world around us. I went around whispering this until I gained the courage to mention it to Kirkland. With eyes, voice, and heart, he told me to start shouting this—that food is hip-hop, in that the two are doing similar work. Kirkland gave me the confidence to be inventive and to add new ingredients to the classroom batter. I began planning a Food Lit class that first summer at Bread Loaf. Kirkland's echo is all over this work.

Michael Armstrong is also in this book. Michael's legendary Describing the Imagination course at Bread Loaf taught me what it means to see our children as artists and our children's "work" as works of art. As teachers, we can paint with curiosity, imagination, and creativity to yield possibility, topography, and magic for our students. Michael Armstrong was a masterpiece.

The summer following Michael's class, I had the opportunity to take Jennifer Wicke's Critical Writing class at Bread Loaf. I wrote "Say Yes to Pears" (see Chapter 1) in her class. She wrote, "You are a writer" at the top of the page. When I told her about writing more about food lit, she told me with her words and eyes and heart, "You have to!" Professor Wicke is the reason I have continued to write about teaching.

I also credit the all-star team of teachers in the Writing and Acting for Change course at Bread Loaf. Jackie Jones Royster's writing anchored the class and charged our group to think about what it means to be "critically conscious" as teachers, as rhetoricians, and as people. Professors Dixie Goswami, Andrea Lunsford, John Elder, Beverly Moss, and Laurie Patton challenged our group to think about our capacity to make change through "collective genius." They encouraged us to be visionaries and to see how we can aspire, in Andrea Lunsford's words, "to allow our writing to move off the page and go and make change in the world."

Dixie Goswami has taught me that the challenges worth taking on are the ones that scare you the most, and that what propels you is not only the belief of others in you, but also knowing that your work is for others. The true thing that makes change happen is creating community and being part of a caring community like the Middlebury Bread Loaf School of English and the Bread Loaf Teacher Network. When you believe in community, you realize that the credit belongs to all the people who believe in you and whose echoes you carry with you.

I would also like to thank Houston Barber, Nathan Meyer, and Rebecca Nicolas, principals at FCHS, along with all our administration, counselors, staff, parents, and students at FCHS; our FCHS Alumni Association; the C.E. and S. Foundation; the Cralle Foundation; the Ford Foundation; the Academy for Teachers; the Write to Change Foundation; Jefferson County Public Schools; NCTE; Middlebury College, the Middlebury Breadloaf School of English, and the Middlebury Bread Loaf Teacher Network; and all people and communities that have encouraged and supported Joe and me in this journey. Joe and I would like to thank our student editors, Courtney Ellis and Trey Hughes, along with all who have submitted writing, time, and encouragement to *Say Yes to Pears* along the way.

Finally, I would like to thank my wife, Emily, as well as our children, Elliot and Stella, for their constant support and belief. They are my greatest inspirations.

Saying Yes

Saying Yes to This Story (Joe Franzen)

Telling this story has been difficult. It didn't happen in a predictable, linear fashion, making the organization of the book a challenge of whether to tell our story chronologically, by student, by strategy, by class; . . . whimsy, a prince, chickens, pumpkins, sausage, and a failing school all shaped the unpredictable, web-like evolution of a program that is a mash-up of culinary arts, English, agriculture, environmental studies, philosophy, community activism, social studies, and just about everything those disciplines touch. Funding for these projects came from the Centers for Disease Control, alumni, local foundations and philanthropies such as the C.E. and S. Foundation, school budgets, produce sales, fundraisers, parents, and our own back pockets. Permission for these endeavors was often undertaken on faith that no one would get hurt, and then bequeathed once the project was successfully completed. We use the name "Food Studies program" to encompass a series of classes (Food Lit; Food Sociology; Global Issues I, II, and Advanced; Cooking Club; Cooking 101; and Environmental Club); the community of students, teachers, and partners who participated in each project; and the adventures of this community from the garden to the Navajo Nation (https://navajokentuckians.com/) from 2010 to 2017. We know that our story is specific to the time, place, and context of a "failing" school in Louisville, Kentucky, starting in 2010.

Having acknowledged this, however, what we experienced is something incredibly transferable to every classroom, teacher, student, and school: how to say yes. By saying yes, we were led along well-worn paths of inquiry learning and bushwhacked into new jungles of interdisciplinary learning. We hope that you, through reading the many voices in this book, see the narratives, recipes, lessons, curriculum, and pictures as a framework you can adapt to your school, classroom, and world. This first chapter describes how we started along this path by saying yes to ourselves and the opportunities around us.

Say Yes to Pears: Where Sharing Food Stories Can Lead (Brent Peters)

We write the word *food* on a piece of paper. Around it, we write all the glorious, revelatory, embarrassing, gross, and sometimes painful associations we have with food. We include the places and people who are connected to our food memories. The paper fills up quickly. Then we share. Nick is learning to make his grandpa's legendary peanut butter fudge. Blanca shares her family's tradition of making El Salvadorian pupusas on Sunday nights and the accompanying call to her grandmother in San Salvador. Kenny teaches us about bubble tea from Vietnam, offers to bring in pho and rambutans. Ivy tells us that her grandmother has a load of organic pears from the trees in her yard—that her dad just harvested them—and she can bring them in. Tomorrow. She has already texted her mom. Yes.

The first day of Food Lit proves to me that you can have a meal without any food, and that a word can be food. Our first class is a dinner table: we laugh, tell stories, and listen carefully. Our stories remind us of places, people, and tastes, actions that are in season in the territories of memory. We are filled with 50 pounds of compelling pear stories.

I meet Ivy's mom in front of school the next morning when the driveway is a parade of brake lights and quick good-byes—a balancing act of book bags and warm drinks. She jumps out of the car. I introduce myself and then help her open the car's trunk. As I heave the pears up, I watch the car visibly stand up from relief of the weight on the shocks. Wow, thank you so much. Thank you, she says. These pears would have gone to waste.

When you have 50 pounds of pears and a strict lesson plan, pears go to waste. You also get fruit flies. Which are gross. But pear butter, pear chutney, pear sauce, dried pears, and pear apple almond muffins are not gross, especially when a class works together to peel, core, and

Ivy with her tub of pears in the busy hallway.

research pear recipes. We experiment, and we mess up . . . a lot. But messing up is how we get to all our delicious discoveries. And delicious discoveries lead us to lots of leftovers. We have enough pear creations to share with other students and staff, and we have enough of a shared experience to sustain a collective memory. We add a common reference point to our food maps—Ivy's grandma's pears. We are now on a journey together. And we are learning in season.

In the food world, awareness surrounds what is local and seasonal. Pears are in season in the fall; so are the apples in our small orchard at FCHS and in the surrounding orchards in Kentucky and southern Indiana. Greens like kale, chard, and collards are going haywire in the FCHS garden. Radishes pop up out of the soil and look like lollipops, carrots are popsicles, beets are bulls-eyes, and cilantro are like silky miniature palm trees. The last tomatoes announce themselves in full, splitting from late rain. Some call them seconds; we call them eat-them-nows. Butternut and acorn squash hide behind leaves and winding vines. Pumpkins bulge, as do cantaloupes and watermelons. Can we harvest some of these vegetables and have a class meal? Yes. We'll save the gourds for table decoration. And let's invite Ivy's grandmother as a way of saying thank you. Do you think she will say . . . yes?

Food Lit class processing Ivy's pears.

We do harvest these vegetables, and we prepare them with care for our first class meal. Roasted veggie burritos, tomato mole, a mixed green salad with watermelon, cucumbers, and a vanilla vinaigrette. We place them all on one big table, set up just outside the school entrance. Before we eat, we write. The prompt: What is a meal? During our meal, we talk about many things, but one of them is what a meal is and isn't for us. Our definitions are as multidimensional as we are.

We create the definition of what we want a meal to be when we have one together, and we return to our classroom with more than just a meal. The meal has made us hungry for a classroom where we all are in season. This realization goes deeper than the core of the pear, further than the core of a table conversation, and beyond the Common Core State Standards; we are caring for the core of our identity by learning that what we care about and who we care about matters.

Ivy's gran does join our class meal. She says she had no idea all of this was happening at school. "And this is an English class, right?"

"Yes. Food Lit."

"Okay. It's just that Ivy was explaining this, and I was having trouble understanding how it all connected. Now I see. Food and English. You are doing more than just being in a class."

"What else do you see?"

Ivy's grandmother supplied the class with 50 lbs. of pears, then joined us for a class meal.

"I see a lot of kids forming a community. I see that food is an unlimited metaphor. I see a classroom that looks like a family. And everyone looks hungry."

When we consume any food item, we are eating the story of that thing. When we eat one of Ivy's pears, we eat the season, and we eat water, soil, land, weather, pollination, and family story. When we work in our school garden and eat from it, we take a bite out of our school. We become Fern Creek High School in a deep and philosophical way. One Food Lit philosopher's thoughts led to this question: If we eat from the garden and are Fern Creek, what are we when we eat school lunch? Well, we are more than dough, cheese, tomatoes, fruit salad, ranch dressing, plastic forks, styrofoam trays, garbage bags, compost bins, frozen-then-reheated, boxed-then-shipped; we are more than forgotten on the bus; more than nothings; we are far more than growling tummies; we are even more than homemade. We are creative, critical readers and writers who can take on big questions and read the world for the answers. If we can read a garden, then we can read a cafeteria. We can read the farmers market and the grocery store, the concession stand, and the vending machine. We *should* read these things, because they are part of us, part of our day, and part of our identity.

By extension, when we make a cup of tea to go with our pear apple almond muffins, we become part of the tea's story—its history, its location, and all the hands that went into making it. An almond connects us to the Central Valley in California—to bees, drought, hydrology, monoculture, climate change; to almond farmers and the plight of undocumented workers; to John Steinbeck and the Dust Bowl. A bite of an apple is a bite out of the beginning of the Trojan War, of Atalanta and her golden apples, of the Renaissance Garden of Eden paintings, of resurging heirloom varieties, of genetics, of idioms like "the apple of my eye," of Neruda's odes, and of the Apple technology in our pockets. Food is our connection to the world, our passport full of stamps, our taste of time, language, literature, and culture. Why not say yes to all these connections? In our class, we just said yes to pears, and 50 pounds of possibility followed.

How a Class Says Yes (Joe Franzen)

When trying to encourage the classroom to reflect your ideals, especially when they are counter to the "traditional" roles and forms of the classroom, sometimes you get friction and conflict. With our first group of Food Lit students in the fall of 2011, we often heard "Why does this all have to be about food?" or "I am sick of this food stuff!" These statements challenged us to clarify for ourselves whether we were being innovative and engaging teachers, or, as food nerds ourselves, we were trying to colonize the minds of youth. We had to reach inside ourselves to analyze why we were making the effort to design a new curriculum, challenge classroom norms, and put in hours of extra work to create a lesson that seemed to succeed just a little more than usual.

Many food studies programs are oriented to produce individuals prepared for vocations in farming and the food industry. Some are geared to influence students to decrease body mass index and adopt healthier lifestyles. Some are cloaked cultural manipulation. If a program doesn't have a clear goal at the start, the larger community will try to impose one of these expectations on that program, sometimes to the detriment of the work in the classroom.

We decided we were not out to produce farmers, chefs, skinny children, or vegans. We wanted to empower students to critically engage with every text around them through using food as a contextual theme to understand, explore, engage, and evaluate the world for themselves. If, through that process, they became farmers, chefs, healthy, happy, or vegans, they would be more conscientious, successful, and compassionate than the products of the programs that limit the scope and definition of success in the classroom.

A potential restaurant called Bad Bitches and Champagne helped us greatly in achieving this philosophical goal. The fall 2011 pilot class of Food Lit was a tough group of students. As teachers, we welcomed students into the class and, before closing the door, took a deep breath and steeled ourselves for whatever might happen in the next seventy minutes. In trying to differentiate instruction and engage some of the hidden talent in the class, we started a unit in which students designed and pitched a restaurant to a group of investors. The Restaurant Project, based in entrepreneurship, marketing, business, and research, set up each student as a restaurateur as well as an investor by handing each one a (fake) $5,000 check to invest in the restaurant they saw as the best investment. To sweeten the deal, the group of restaurateurs to reach the needed level of start-up capital would be taken out to dinner by Brent and me. Bad Bitches and Champagne (BBC) won this competition.*

The students needed to prepare three pitchable artifacts for the restaurant, which could include but were not limited to a logo, rendering of the restaurant facade, marketing campaign, sample menu, supplier manifest, budget spreadsheet, architectural schematics of the floor plan, and any other teacher-negotiated expression of talent that would best portray their idea. With this open-ended, project-based task, as well as a multitude of resources (e.g., menus, ads, restaurant ideas, signs) gleaned from the community, before long students were recording jingles, asking whether Louisville had ever had a soul food Korean fusion restaurant, researching market prices for fish and learning about the most visually appealing manta ray. Most important, all students were seriously and personally engaging in this task.

Three students who struggled with literacy skills, attendance, and behavior worked diligently but secretly. Rulers were requested. A foul language variance was filed for. The formula to figure out square footage was researched. Brent and I were largely kept out of the loop. We saw the name "Ray's Fish House" and the gothic-themed farm-to-table concept. We challenged the late-night boxed

---

*We acknowledge the complicated nature of this name with regard to masculine identity, equality, and the system of patriarchy that has oppressed and hindered many in society. We also acknowledge that these young men were often unengaged in school and didn't seem to see their identities represented in the school culture. When they announced the name of their restaurant, Brent and I had some tough conversations: Do we take away their seed money for the demeaning nature of the theme? Do we focus on the use and role of certain words in US society and compromise the success these students felt? By allowing the success, are we condoning a larger system of oppression?

All teachers wade in these waters whether they realize it or not. To have meaningful conversations about empathy, compassion, and understanding in regard to challenging topics, students must feel like they are part of a community in which they have value and something at stake. We erred on the side of building that relationship by proposing that the students might change the name to be more inclusive; however, the first place finish remained. I am sure that some teachers would have navigated these waters differently. Like many—maybe most—teachers, we have made the perfect decision about, and had the perfect conversation with, a student only in hindsight.

dinner concept that seemed thinly tied to the munchies, asking for more details in the menu and marketing. But "BBC," the restaurant that was gaining class notoriety through its secretive nature, remained unexamined and untested by Brent and me.

On presentation day, the three young men of BBC excitedly and proudly volunteered to go first. Each held a large piece of drawing paper with the edges together to build anticipation. Troy started by opening up a rendering of the restaurant facade. Under his big grin, he held a professional drawing of a two-story nightclub/restaurant that would have been at home on the Vegas strip. He talked about the neon outlining of the champagne glass and the script that would be used for the lettering on the sign. He talked about how to copyright the script, logo, and design of the facade for franchising purposes. He described the purpose of the design for security and function, all while the class stared at the purposeful color scheme and crisp straight lines that naturally engaged the eye. Troy presented as a professional, and the quality of the work made a strong case for that ethos.

The next young man opened up the floor plan of the restaurant, which looked like a hand-drawn computer-aided design (CAD) plan. The thought behind the layout demonstrated intentional consideration of flow, use, and potential issues for occasions when crowds of people would come to the restaurant for events and to enjoy themselves. Hands and questions were popping off in the crowd, students eager to know more details: "What does BBC stand for?" "Where is the second-floor layout?" "What is the age to get in?" "What type of performers will be performing?" As professionals, the three restaurateurs and entrepreneurs politely asked the group of investors to please hold their questions till the end of the presentation.

The third artifact, a complete clothing line to accompany the franchised nightclub/restaurant, had students leaning over their desks to look at the detail on the BBC hoodie, critique the placement of the logo on the V-neck, and offer visions of how the merchandise line might expand into its own fashion business. Students demanded to know the name of the restaurant. The three young men looked at Brent and me, and, without knowing what we were going to hear, we nodded yes.

"Bad Bitches and Champagne."

The class went wild, hooting, hollering, clapping, congratulating, and, thankfully, ignoring Brent's and my red cheeks. The three young men settled the class down and, in a masterful piece of marketing, said that the restaurant could only become a reality, and the second-floor layout only be completed, with— "your investor dollars!" With that, they stepped away from the front of the class.

Although the rest of the students' restaurants were amazing, showcasing each student's unique skill set, passion, and ideas, the smiles on the three young men's faces remained throughout the entire class period and into the next day, when the invested capital was announced. By an overwhelming margin, these young men gained enough investment capital to start their restaurant, and Brent and I set a date for dinner at—BBC, an actual restaurant in Louisville except that the acronym stands for Bluegrass Brewing Co. We called home for each of the young men, and after explaining that their sons weren't in trouble, we told their mothers about the boys' success and why it was necessary to take their sons to a restaurant.

I wish I could say that the dinner was a load of laughs, that we broke out of our roles as teachers and students and really got to know one another on personal levels that transformed our relationships in the classroom and resulted in straight As for the budding entrepreneurs and fewer classroom conflicts for us. But I can't. Still, the meal was a win. The chef came out to tell his story to the young men and hear their ideas, which they told with pride. We had a good meal, talked about school, looked at the wall-mounted televisions during awkward silences, and pondered the reality of how our roles as teachers and students so dictated our behaviors that those roles remained even in an environment so different from our classroom.

In reflecting on the Restaurant Project and especially Bad Bitches and Champagne, we realized that those students were not really passionate about being farmers, chefs, or vegans, nor was changing the foods they ate a priority. Maybe some of the pushback we received was because we seemed to be pushing those expectations in our own struggle to find the identity of Food Lit. What those young men needed was a way to feel proud in the classroom, which we finally accomplished by empowering them with the literacies to engage with the world and enrich it through their own personal set of challenges. Brent and I realized that food offers the interconnectivity of every facet of human life. If you are alive, you eat, every day, with other people, different foods, with different messages. We learned that we needed to be the catalyst for exploration through that universal lens of food, and whether those young men became restaurateurs, chefs, entrepreneurs, architects, bouncers, fashion designers, bartenders, public speakers, marketing specialists, or something else, they would be better in any of those roles on account of their Food Lit experience.

The school year ended and so did the pilot class. As with all pilots, one must wait to see how the episode is received before making the next installment. Food Lit could have ended right then, a successful venture in that we tried, we learned, and students were exposed to something outside the traditional

English classroom. Brent and I could have been okay with that, but the students demanded that the class be continued. Those students who had asked why everything had to do with food or said they were sick of all this "food stuff" were now wondering how an English class could even exist without food at its the center. Those students wanted the class to loop up with them for instruction next year. Somehow, Food Lit became an identity for these students. And the administration saw and heard.

Although neither our goal nor our instruction was focused on increasing test scores, that happened in a statistically meaningful way. By getting students engaged and excited about using literacy around food, we were able to help them improve their general literacy skills. For us this was a surprise. We eschewed test prep and using standardized forms of assessment in the class, yet students were able to translate and adapt their literacy skills to various situations, from multiple-choice questions, to talking about "good food," to writing their own food narratives, to working in the garden. Dr. Barber, head administrator at the time, remarked that our "comprehensive" class, the lowest of the three levels of English class, was performing close to the level of our AP-track students.

With the support of students and the administrative team, Brent and I started planning for the next year with a clearer set of goals and expectations, as well as an expanding tool bag for what it meant to be an interdisciplinary food studies teacher. More important, Brent and I realized that Food Lit was more than just an English course; it was the creation of a community of learners who wanted to own something larger than themselves, who wanted to give back to the students who inherited the program, who wanted to see the program grow and flourish.

Say Yes to You (Brent Peters)

You know what is inside of you. You know the ideas you have for your teaching, the changes you imagine in your classroom and new ways of doing things. You know the questions you leave with each day, the challenges you circle back to each school year. You know what growth can and wants to look like. You know what obstacles you face and what drives you to take on these obstacles. You know your community, and you know the place where you live. You know what you love.

In reading *Say Yes to Pears*, you may discover that you want to start a Food Lit class, a Global Issues class, a Food and Sociology class, a Cooking Club, or a Cooking class. You might want to take some of the strategies in this book and make them your own. Or you might see the ideas in the book as sparks inspiring you to create a new strategy, thematic unit, approach to the teaching of reading or writing, or your own themed course. We hope this book inspires you to say yes to you as a teacher—and, more important, to the joy of what saying yes will lead you to do in the classroom.

As you read, we know you will be asking, *How can this all work in my class?*

What follows are not lesson plans that can be plugged into a single day; rather, we share strategies and the story of a pedagogy that is culturally responsive, multidisciplinary, compassion oriented, challenging, and fun. The ideas in this book have taken form over many years. And while Joe and I will cite scholarly work where available, our most important sources of inspiration and scholarship for the ideas in this book have emerged from our experiences in the classroom, from listening to our students at Fern Creek High School, and from Joe and I collaborating and challenging each other over the years in an informal way. What follows are our best versions (up to this point) of strategies and projects that are the result of years of doing, reflecting, refining, and re-doing.

How *Say Yes to Pears* Is Organized (Brent Peters)

Chapter 2 takes you through a year of Food Lit starting with making the case for connecting food to an English class; moving on to the introduction of food maps at the beginning of the year; then working through the major strategies, projects, recipes, and reflections in Food Lit throughout the year; and concluding with a Food Lit framework that we call the Food Lit Flyover. Joe and I designed and co-taught Food Lit at Fern Creek High School for four years. I have continued to teach and expand Food Lit as a sophomore English class at FCHS. While the ideas of Food Lit are based on a strong collaboration between Joe and me, I guide you through a year of Food Lit alongside FCHS students and family members.

In Chapter 3, Joe leads you through how Food Lit looks beyond an English class, through Food and Sociology and Global Issues courses, both food-based, multidisciplinary, project-based classes that expand both what is possible in a class and the physical location of a class (e.g., a school garden, the city of Louisville, a food lab, etc.). Joe shares strategies, project ideas, narratives, recipes and flyovers, guiding questions, and so on. Joe is joined throughout Chapter 3 by students who share narratives, reflections, and recipes that speak to the impact of pedagogical approaches related to Food Lit. Chapter 3 builds to the expansion of Food Lit beyond the school day, with the culminating stories and recipes of the book being about the creation and development of the FCHS Garden and Cooking Clubs.

Joe and I are teachers, and we wrote this book based on our experiences as teachers who do the work of teachers, every day. We believe in teachers and the work of teachers. Our aim in sharing this book with you is *not* to prove that we have figured everything out over the years; rather, it's to show our efforts to become better teachers every day for our kids. The book is written in this spirit of pursuing the growth that we are all seeking as teachers.

2

Saying Yes to Food Lit

A lady who writes, and whom I admire very much, wrote me that she learned from Flaubert that it takes at least three activated sensuous strokes to make an object real; and she believes that this is connected with our having five senses. If you're deprived of any of them, you're in a bad way, but if you're deprived of more than two at once, you almost aren't present.

—*Flannery O'Connor*, "The Nature and Aim of Fiction"

Food Lit is not like any other English Class. You don't sit and read out of a grammar book all day. With this class you actually get to have fun while learning. All of the hands-on activities we do actually helps us on how we see things in everyday life. This class helps you connect and analyze things on a deeper level.

—*Chyniah B.*, 2016 Food Lit Alum.

We All Eat: The Case for Food Lit

We all eat, right? What Joe and I are doing in even thinking about a Food Lit class is considering what is already in our classroom, as well as how "a great deal of what happens in-school is born beyond it" (Kirkland 10). Food is one such thing. What do our students generally all have with them on any given day? Food. What do we have tucked in our desk drawers? Food. What are our kids generally not looking forward to eating? School lunch. What are we generally not looking forward to eating? School lunch. So we've got a place of promise and an immediate deficit that we can make up in a Food Lit course. And we've got a way to build community immediately by inviting everyone to bring in food—not just what students have in their backpacks (think about that bag of Takis, those Cheetos, that bag of Starburst Minis), but what we can make and bring in for everyone (think of your favorite dish from home, think staying after school to make cakes or corn bread for class). We can also do something that has brought people together for years and years and years—share a meal, at a table. We can *look at one another, in the eyes,* and get to know each other and enjoy one another's company—and even begin to look forward to seeing each other.

I am not much different from any other teacher in my desire to create a strong classroom community. And I am kidding myself if I think that my story is unique in terms of having a connection to food. We all do. We all have food stories and deep connections to the world through the foods we buy, grow, remember, cook, eat, throw away, give away, and let go bad. As Flannery O'Connor suggests in the first chapter epigraph, food also makes us feel alive by encouraging a wondrous sensory overlap (69). We are all cooks in some way, and we all have powerful food memories that connect to people, places, and significant moments and times in our lives. We all eat and drink and have appetites and cravings as well as deep connections to smell and taste and combinations of foods. We all shop, have brand preferences, and we all make impulse buys, too. And based on where we live, our food stories and the land and landscape tell much different stories that are deeply woven into our identity and sense of place—sometimes so much so that we forget to name these stories because we tend to take them as a given.

Now that I have been out of the kitchen for a while, I see how what I am going for in the classroom and what I went for in the kitchen are very much the same. I want to prepare a great lesson that will be memorable for my kids. I want them to enjoy being in my class, and I want them to feel part of a story and feel better about themselves by having been a part of a supporting and joyful environment. I want them to feel that they have a seat at any table in any room. And I want them to look forward to coming back to school and to class, and I want them to come back hungry!

If literature and stories are all about people (and other living things), then as teachers we are dealing with living things who are also connected to food. Food is a lens of sorts—to read the literary world and our world (in the Freirean sense) to see who is eating, who is not eating, who and what does it take to produce the food we eat, and at what expense. As Dan Jurafsky suggests, food is its own language that "tells us about human psychology, who we are, from the nature and perceptions and emotions to the social psychology of our attitudes toward others" (5). Food connects us to those around us, but we can take our connection a step further—we can look at food as a way to consider and connect to people we don't know by taking the imaginary leap to connect to the supply chain of the products we buy, all the people who are connected to that supply chain, as well as all the characters and narrators we meet in stories, novels, and poems.

When I explain Food Lit to English teachers, I say the following: Food Lit is a multidisciplinary English class where we use food as a lens and an invitation to read the world around us. We work in our class garden; we have class meals; we cook together, read food as a text, do food and text pairings, create our own town, and read and write a lot while forming a class community that is much like a family at a dinner table.

I generally get an enthusiastic response, and then I get the inevitable question you may be asking right now: *What do you read?* I know these teachers are thinking (because they've told me) that all the texts we read will be food-related texts, but that isn't the case. I tell them we read *The Great Gatsby* and *Othello*; *The Kite Runner, The Piano Lesson, A Raisin in the Sun,* and *The Old Man and the Sea*; *The Botany of Desire* and *The Odyssey*. "Oh. Are those food texts?"

Yes.

And then I tell them that all texts are food texts in some way. I describe how we do food and text pairings in a strategy called Campfire, about our class meals and teas, and about how we work in our school garden. It's not so much that we eat together to eat, or work in the garden to work, but that we do these things to see how a meal, a garden, a grocery store, a seed packet, a cereal box, a Thanksgiving turkey, or a chocolate bar can be a text that can be read and can connect us—to our community, to our world, to finding out who we are and to finding out who other people are. As Andrea Lunsford suggests, food texts make arguments, too, and bring us into the argument: "The clothes you wear, the foods you eat, and the groups you join make nuanced, sometimes unspoken assertions about who you are and what you value" (5). Opening the door to allow food into the classroom encourages connections to happen that this book can only begin to describe and that, I promise, you will be able to make and create much better than Joe and I because you know your kids, your community, your school, and you know what you teach better than anyone does.

In what follows, I wish to share some of the things that have worked in our Food Lit class, along with simple recipes and suggestions about how you might make this course your own. Much like a recipe, change it a bit to suit your taste, add or subtract a few ingredients. The class is not a health class or a referendum on healthy eating (although health, wellness, and good/bad food come up in class); it's a class that allows the texts already in your and your students' lives to be in the class and in the conversation in a new way. Food Lit is also an invitation to open the door to reach out to the world (including holding class outside) and to make room for serendipitous occasions and connections that will happen as a result of letting food in.

Food is a metaphor as much as a lens in the classroom, so letting both the word *food* and food itself become the focus creates the conditions that allow the class to become more like a dinner table—where everyone shares, listens, and laughs, and where knowledge moves around the room. I didn't always want to be in a classroom listening to a teacher teach, but there were very few dinner tables I didn't want to be a part of. What follows can help you and your students bring more of yourselves *into* the room, be more *yourselves* each day, and leave with a sense of belonging that is large enough to be something you and your students can look forward to.

Each of the strategies discussed in this chapter connects to one or more of these three aims of Food Lit:

1. To read food as a text on its own as well as next to and inside of literature to gain a greater understanding of and connection to various literary texts, and to develop our abilities to think critically and creatively

2. To read food as a way to connect us to our stories and identity, our home, our community, and the world around us

3. To read food as an invitation to build community—as a way to "do" (*as in a class working in the school garden and/or cooking together*), to "create" (*as in writing a food narrative or creating a class town*), and to "invite" (*as in hosting a good food class meal and bringing in our families*)

Questions to Chew On

1. How does food figure into the novels, essays, plays, poems, and other texts you teach?

2. How is food a lens through which you could look at the topics and texts you teach? (For instance, in Chapter 5 of *The Great Gatsby*, Nick hosts a tea for Gatsby and Daisy and serves lemon cakes. What would the class be able to notice in this chapter after serving tea and lemon cake in class? How could the group connect to the text and to Nick, Daisy, and Gatsby after joining them for the tea? How is this scene more than just a tea? And what is each of the characters hungry for besides tea? What new writing possibilities could emerge for your students from the experience?)

3. What food-related issues do you talk about in class? What food-related issues are specific to your community or geographic region?

4. Does a lesson or thematic unit that you teach invite a food connection via food products or to global events that are connected to food production, food culture, or global supply chain?

5. Which of your food stories that are about more than food could you share with your class? How can you invite students to tell stories related to food, or to find out or critique the stories of the foods they consume?

6. Is there a time of the year when a class potluck would be appropriate for your class? What is the simplest way to host a class potluck? Is there a question or a theme around which a potluck could be organized?

7. Do you have a space where you could cook with your class in school, either during or after school?

How This Chapter Is Organized

In this chapter, I share an entire school year of Food Lit strategies and activities. Although the topics and what we read and write in class change from year to year, the essential strategies of the class don't change, and I present them in the order in which they happen throughout the year. The order is deliberate in that it is designed with the community in mind: lower stakes strategies such as food maps and Garden Wisdom at the beginning, higher stakes strategies like Panzenland, which depend on the established trust of the community, closer to the end of the year. Some strategies, such as class meals (we usually have three class meals per year) and Campfire, happen throughout the year. Others, like the Curiosity + Challenge Project, happen only once.

I take you through the year by sharing an explanation of the strategy, followed by either a recipe for performing the strategy or an example of student work, as well as some reflection questions along the way.

I want to share how class starts with an invitation to tell stories and how that invitation builds and grows community. I have tried to pare down the course into the most essential strategies. By sharing the strategies and examples of what we have done in class, I invite you to do them, too—in your individual way—with your own text pairings and themes, and with your own spin and personality, sharing them in turn with your students so that they can own these strategies, too. In addition to taking you through a year of Food Lit, I provide a "flyover" of the year that provides a closer look at how the strategies work within the big picture of the class, including some of the texts we read and the writings we compose throughout the year. Here is the progression of Chapter 2:

Food Maps and Food Narratives—We start our class by naming our connections with food and writing narratives that are about more than food.

Class Meal—We bring home to school by bringing in our favorite dishes and building a class family in the first few weeks of school.

Class in the Garden—We pair Garden Wisdom quotes with our class experience in the garden while everything is in full bloom in the fall.

Campfire—Our Food Lit literature circle begins with a food and text pairing. This starts the first weeks of school and runs throughout the year.

Curiosity + Challenge Project—This project constitutes the homework we have always wished for and a solution to boredom over the winter break.

Class Tea—This activity is a way to warm up in winter and to celebrate Valentine's Day.

Panzenland—The class creates a town in the spring to debate an issue, use argumentation skills, and have a theatrical experience.

Food Lit Flyovers—I provide an overview of a Food Lit year to see how all these strategies work thematically and with reading and writing tasks.

Food Maps

It was with a deep understanding of the interwoven layers of food and story that Joe and I decided to begin our Food Lit class by encouraging students to share their food stories. We ask students to go to the places in their memories that show their full selves, and we ask simply that they list the ingredients of their memories—the sounds, the people, the dishes, the places, the failures, the lessons, the favorites, the confessions, the gross encounters, the losses, and the celebrations they have had around food. We call this creation a food map. The food map idea was inspired by Nancie Atwell's heart map idea from *Lessons That Change Writers*. We write the word *food* in the center of a piece of paper, and then we list all of the things that surround this word.

We get laughs, smiles, blushes, sadness, vulnerabilities, invitations, awkwardness, kindness, and character all at the same time. We harvest the beginnings of stories that are inside of us, just waiting to be shared, validated, fact-checked by family, and brought to the surface, dusted off, and held up to the light to shine. When we share the snippets, we help others remember the time when . . . and experience lots of that-makes-me think-of-that-one-time-when moments. We share our maps during the first days of school and then return to them to see which of the items on the food map is a story that is about *more than* food. We see that food is an invitation to connect to stories and to share stories. Then we read food narratives like Marcus Samuelsson's "Face to Face with Fugu" from *A Fork in the Road* by James Oseland and student narratives like Milo Q's "The Guilt of Biscuits and Gravy" (which follows) to begin the journey to write our narratives that tell the limitless and generous stories of us, or, in Thomas Newkirk's words, to construct "causal narratives [that] allow us to imagine ourselves as agents, even heroes, in our own stories, which can be purposeful and coherent" (28). When we share these stories, the students listen intently, as if in the sharing we are all being fed, all connecting, and starting to see the depths of one another.

Food Map Recipe: You Try

Take our first word *food* and try this for yourself, maybe with a friend. Maybe you could try to write a food map right now. We will give you the question stems and a few model food maps. See what you might be able to discover. Fix a coffee or a tea. Turn on some music. Think about your favorite soup or your mom's chicken and dumplings, or those cinnamon rolls that your grandma used to burn on Sunday mornings, how when you have a burned cinnamon roll now you get a frog in your throat. Think about your grandpa's bean soup with a ham hock that he seasoned with ketchup, or your grandpa frying catfish on the back porch with the high-pitched droning and whirring sound of homemade vanilla ice cream spinning—the icy, grainy kind that gives you brain freeze and announces summer. Think about the bags of Oreos and egg sandwiches wrapped in wax

Sample of Jada's food map.

paper that your grandma used to sneak into your tackle box when you went fishing.

Think about your favorite snacks, your food obsessions, your food quirks, like cinnamon in your coffee, or unlikely pairs, like lavender and tomatoes, fresh mint and scrambled eggs, strawberries and fresh ginger. Think about your food confessions, like the time you made a peanut butter and tuna fish sandwich because that was all you could find in the cabinet, or the time you ate a dog biscuit to see what it tasted like. Think about holidays, campfire food, and your bagged lunch with a soda can wrapped in aluminum foil. Don't forget the note from your mom in the bag and the potato chips that tasted like bananas because they were in the same bag.

Don't be a chicken. Try it. Then bring your food map with you when you do this activity with your class. You'll be at the table together. You'll see how each person is weird and complex in his or her own way. And there will be some deep emotion, too. All it takes is the word *food*.

◎ ◎ ◎ ◎

Ingredients:

1 blank sheet of paper
1–10 colored markers
1 creative mind
1 narrative built around food

To Start:

- Grab a marker and a piece of paper.
- On your paper, write the word *food*.
- Think about this word and write about your own relationship to food.

Question Stems for Class:

What do you think of when you hear the word *food*?

What specific foods are important for you?

What connections to people, places, events, memories, holidays, and ceremonies do you associate with food?

What are your favorite foods and drinks? What dishes and preparations of food are specific to you, your family, and your friends?

Think about and write down your food confessions, guilty pleasures, weaknesses, weird food combinations. Add visuals if you like.

Fill the page with all your connections with food. Share these and add to this map as necessary. Instead of writing "peanut butter cookies," write "Grandpa's gooey peanut butter cookies." The specifics are where the stories come alive!

◎ ◎ ◎ ◎

When we finish our food maps, we develop a couple of the memories included on the maps. We ask kids to think about which of the food items on their maps are about more than food. Which ones are a story? Then we tell that story, bringing out *how* the food item is about more than food.

From Food Map to Food Narrative: Our First Class Writing

Once Joe and I complete our food maps, we share them with each other and with the class. We find out a lot about ourselves and about others. Our first writing task in the class is to choose from our food maps the two or three things that have an emotional pull and a big story connected to them. We ask the big question: Which one of these food items is about much more than food? We write informally about a few of these food items to explore the story connected to each and to choose the one that we want to become our food narrative.

Then we write and share our food narratives. Reading them aloud in class is optional, but when students are through the draft stage, we make time in class to read the narratives to the whole group. When we share them, we discover that food and our memories of food can tell a big story—sometimes funny, sometimes sad, sometimes serious, etc.—that helps us let other people into our lives. What follows is a narrative by Milo Q., who isn't one of the first people to speak in a room and admits to being shy. When Milo shared this narrative, not only did the classroom change because Milo felt accepted and part of the community, but also Milo heard the following words for the first time: *You are a writer.* Through writing these food narratives, we make the case that we are in a room full of writers who not only belong in the space, but also have a lot to teach and learn from one another, and that our stories match or exceed the complexity of the literature we will be reading throughout the course of the year. Milo's narrative makes this clear. As bell hooks states, we build community "by sharing and receiving one another's stories; it is a ritual of communion that opens our minds and our hearts. Sharing in ways that help us connect, we come to know each other better" (52). We start to become a learning community by becoming a reading and writing community where telling and listening to stories is valued and part of our identity.

Student Narrative: The Guilt of Biscuits and Gravy (Milo Q.)

Sometimes I would join him in those early morning breakfasts after I had pulled an all-nighter sitting at the laptop. Those mornings were all the same: sitting near the double-door entrance in a booth with country music playing softly in the background while we had our plastic trays of steaming food sitting in front of us. I would always order soggy pancakes with no butter and a side of bacon; Jim would have two biscuits completely submerged in gravy.

Jim sat across from me each time I joined him for breakfast, enabling me to have a good look at his kind face. He was lean, tall, and tan with a tint of red to his cheeks. Jim's gray-blue eyes always looked tired, but soft. What I remember most is his scarred hands from working day and night as an architect.

In late June of 2012, Jim was diagnosed with cancer. He had a tumor in a vital part of his brain and alongside it, lung cancer due to his long years of smoking. He was with my mom when she told me a couple days later. I was eleven, and I still didn't know how to respond to such a tragedy. I didn't cry or show any emotion at all. I simply nodded and said a quiet "okay" before going on with life as if nothing had changed.

Milo's food map … with "biscuits and gravy" at the bottom.

Before Jim was diagnosed, he built an extra garage in our backyard. While it was being built, I remember playing in a large pile of sand and gravel used for the concrete. Once finished, the garage took up half of the backyard. I had no problem with it of course. I never needed much room to play. Now the garage still stands high and mighty, holding the many memories I have shared with Jim over the years.

That garage was Jim's own man cave that he shared with me; he shared everything in the garage with me. He shared his tools, chairs, his gigantic radio, and the dartboard above it. Jim even shared the experience of building. I sat nearby and watched him build a dollhouse, a bat house, a birdhouse, a swing set, and an elevated fort with a green slide. Most of the things he had built were for me. They were signs of affection for the little girl he had helped raise and taught everything he knew. Despite being my father figure, I never managed to call him dad.

One day a while after Jim was diagnosed, I was sitting in the garage on my favorite stool that stood tall with a cushioned, rotating seat that would let out a shrill squeak whenever you spun. Jim sat in a blue lawn chair that leaned so far back to the point he was practically laying. Although he had lung cancer, he held a cigarette between his chapped lips, blowing smoke through his nostrils like an angry bull.

"How long do you have?" I asked, turning the top of the stool to face him.

Jim paused before he spoke in his deep, gravelly voice, "About four years." To me, four years felt like plenty of time.

"I'm going to miss you."

"I'm going to miss you too," he replied with a sad smile.

Jim's appearance began to change a lot due to the radiation therapy done to keep the cancer cells at bay. He paled and began to lose weight. His hair had started to fall out, leaving him with long, white, thin hair that he refused to cut. Although he didn't look like himself anymore, Jim would still leave the house if he had the strength to. He would even go out in the morning for his biscuits and gravy.

Eventually, he wasn't able to get them anymore. Eventually, he stopped leaving the house, or getting out of bed. Getting up for daily tasks would exhaust him, but he still managed to take care of his bodily functions.

As his condition got worse, Hospice got involved. The nurses would only stop by to make sure he died comfortably and to take notes on his condition. I would sometimes curiously watch them from the doorway of his bedroom.

I remember my Mom going over the procedure of what to do if something happened to him. We had put his patient information and the Hospice phone number on the fridge. She told me to call the number, give Jim's patient I.D, and to wait for their arrival. My mom couldn't stress enough for me not to call 911. They would be required to take him to the hospital and try to help him, but Jim didn't want that. By that point, there was no helping him.

A day before August 9th, 2015, I was standing in the bathroom doorway. The Hospice nurses were in Jim's room, helping him up to his feet and out of bed. My mom stood in the bedroom doorway and I joined her. "What's going on?" I asked with my brows pushed together. My mom didn't look at me.

"They're taking him away, so say bye to Jim." Her sad tone gave me the confirmation that Jim was leaving us. The both of us backed out of the doorway, and I stood in the bathroom doorway again as Jim was guided out into the narrow hall.

Call him Dad. It could be all he's ever wanted to hear from me. I opened my mouth, but hesitated. I said exactly what I didn't want to say as if I had no control over it: "Bye, Jim." He didn't say anything. He probably couldn't. Jim shuffled past the bathroom with the nurses and I moved back into my bedroom. I felt that it was too late to fix my mistake. I got angry with myself and I didn't do anything about it. I just lay on my bed, staring at the starry walls that we had painted together, awaiting the bad news.

The next day, Jim had passed. I didn't sit with my mom and cry; instead, I isolated myself in my room. Even then I had no idea on how to react. I went on with things; did school work without problems, and I talked to my friends. The only time I showed any sort of emotion about my loss was a breakdown in art class due to thinking about him. Now I look back and I feel some emotion, but I still haven't figured out why I never got myself to call him dad.

From Food Narratives to Class Meal

After sharing our food maps and our food narratives, I remember getting the question: *Can you have a meal without food? Because I think we just did.* What flows naturally from opening the door to the classroom as a dinner table is the invitation to look again at the food map and bring in an item from it as part of a class potluck. Joe and I have done this first class meal in a number of ways (as I will share below), but the potluck seems to be the best model for a first class meal because you can do it easily without needing access to a kitchen.

We know that food tells stories, and by bringing in items from the food maps, we find a way onto one another's food maps and into one another's stories as well. We have a meal with food, and with fun, too, and in so doing, we create a way of being together that takes us beyond what any set of class rules could accomplish. After a class meal, students make the case that the communal meal creates an experience for everyone that is much larger than any one individual could achieve.

Class Meal—Collective Joy

If you want to have a successful class meal, start about two weeks before the actual event . . . with an invitation. The invitation can be formal, as in a slip of paper with the date and other relevant information, or it can be a piece of legal paper that gets passed around the room with two columns, one for names and one for the food each individual will bring. Sometimes we add a third column, for "who" you are bringing, for our family class meals.

You pass that list out every day and soon, next to the names, "IDK" gets crossed out and replaced with **Hoppin' John, Three Bean Chili,** and **Memol's Chicken and Dumplins** in bold letters. Each day we take a second to anticipate what the meal will be like and to eat these dishes in our imaginations. Then come the serious questions that let me know that students have communicated with home, that they are working out the logistics on their own:

"How many people are in this class, Mr. Peters?"

"Is anyone allergic to nuts?"

"Would you all like chocolate or vanilla cake? Can we take a vote?"

"Can I bring my dad? My grandma? My mom? My bowling coach? My pastor?"

"Can I bring a Crock-Pot?"

"Is there any way to heat up lasagna?"

"Can I bring drinks? Plates? Cups?"

The list becomes a conversation, a living document of an approaching experience that we are creating together, an unintentional competition between classes of whose meal will be the most delicious. Joe and I say to our groups that the success of the class meal is dependent on how much energy we put into creating an experience, and we place this experience into our students' hands.

Then, maybe a week before the meal, I start asking questions: "Who can bring plates? Cups? Napkins? Who can stay to help decorate the room? Would you mind cutting some flowers? Any chance you could run out to the garden to pick some gourds for the table settings? Who can make a class meal playlist? Who can bring a football? A Frisbee? A volleyball? Who could stay after school on the day of the meal to help make sure the room is clean and to help me move the tables back?"

And the list fills up with the contributions of students. In some cases, their work is what they bring instead of a dish—and this offering is celebrated just as much as any dish a student brings.

When the day of the class meal arrives, you can tell yourself you have a lesson plan—and you might believe that you do—but your lesson plan will really be "have faith." On your way to school on the morning of the class meal, you will be nervous and tired, like you were your first year of teaching when you lived on coffee and cough drops. You will be boiled-down excitement with a large to-do list. It helps to have kids arrive early to check in their classmates' dishes and to put the afternoon dishes in a refrigerator for reheating later. You might want to tag the dishes as they arrive, or set up a folding table for each class period to keep things streamlined.

Generally, we set up long tables around the perimeter of the room so that we can have the first two class meals set up and ready, and then reset later for

Bringing the garden in for a class meal.

the afternoon meals. It's most important to have a cleaning station set up somewhere in the room (maybe around the perimeter) that includes at least two large trash cans, a wash tub (for spills and for washing off tables), a compost bucket (for the chickens), a container for recycling, and a bin for dishes that need washing. When the kids start arriving for class, it's also good to have a specific place for bags and coats so that the floor area stays uncluttered.

By the time the first bell rings, whatever tiredness you felt earlier has turned to joy, and your room has transformed into a restaurant of sorts—a really nice restaurant—and you will begin to wonder, given all your students' help, whether you had anything to do with the setup. You will know that your lesson ("have faith") has been successful when students know that they are responsible for one another's fun. Your room is now "their room," and today they will teach you how "be joyful" is also part of your lesson plan. You will also see the beginnings of deep relief in your students' eyes—their long stares aren't due to the fact that today will be a "fun" day; rather, they're already trying to figure out how every day can be like today. You are secretly considering this, too. With all the activity, though, your answer may as yet be unclear.

Now that things are ready, you must bring order to a hungry crowd, even while the enticing smells create a sense of urgency.

But you can't dive in to eating just yet or you'll miss out on a great opportunity—for patience, for celebration, for a class to be able to name its source of accomplishment, for voices to share exactly what they are offering to the group. There will be interruptions. There will be the late dish arrival accompanied by a grandparent. There will be the wandering students who want to drop in to class because you're never more interesting to them than on class meal day. There will be the student who arrives in tears and needs to talk. It's all okay—your kids will forgive you because you will be deeply human to them today in a way that you haven't yet been. They will see you at your most generous today—and they will like what they see.

Unbeknownst to the kids, I usually bring two surprises in my back pocket. One is a slideshow (or a photo booth video) that I will play at the end of the meal, and the other is an invitation to play outside after the meal (think cornhole, football, Ultimate Frisbee). Both of these surprises are optional, but they will bring joy full circle while also allowing you time to reset the room (with student help) for the next meal.

So what is the plan, the agenda for today? And what state or national standards does a class meal cover for the curious teacher next to you? One part

Class meal in full swing. Dig in, Devin!

of the agenda is community, cooperation, discussion, reflection, care, a greater understanding and appreciation of each individual as a deep text we are getting to know. And, of course, fun.

Your "measurable" standards ("have faith" and "be joyful") are not as important for this day as they are for the next day, the next week, the next month, and the rest of the year. The focus targets of a class meal are care and community. These two things lead to collective joy, to engagement, to risk taking, and to your original lesson plan of having faith being projected back at you in the form of the faith your students will have in you moving forward and the willingness they now have to see you as a person—a vulnerable, sometimes awkward, funny person—who makes mistakes and who is . . . real. A class meal makes a classroom a real place for students, and it makes the room a place they want to be, a place they can be at home inside. That will help you with whatever official standard you are working on in the next day's lesson.

Really, the only way to have a class meal is to decide how you want to do one, and then go for it!

The Cleanup

When the class meal ends, you will be tired in the best kind of way. You will also have some cleanup to do, so it's best to find out who can stay to help. I find that the cleanup doesn't take long if I make sure that all the food disappears first. Either give it away to the students, wrap up any extra for an informal lunch option the next day, or have kids cart it home. A lot of students will peek their heads in during this time, so stay focused and get the job done.

Once the room is back to its original order, you will wonder—just as the kids will the next day—whether the class meal really happened. It did. And you and your kids now have a shared memory and a shared experience. You also are now on one another's food maps. If you've planned ahead, you'll have a few photos to lead off with the next day so that students can see how all the meals went. One of the most important things we do is reflect on everything that happened during the meal. Just as earlier we all had varying definitions of what a meal is, we all saw different and interesting things going on during the meal that, when shared, will give words to the experience and make the case for you and the class to start planning the next meal. Because you've started something, be ready for the question that will become a constant: "When are we going to have our next class meal?"

Next Day Class Meal Reflection Questions

1. Why did we have a class meal? Make an argument. (Think of the opposition too.)

2. What did you learn today during the meal (about yourself, someone else, etc.)? Explain.

3. Write about something you noticed about the class meal that no one else did. Be insightful.

Some Options: Ways You Could Do Your First Class Meal

As described in the "Collective Joy" section, the first class meal of the year is usually a potluck, but here are some other approaches we have taken to our first class meal. If you don't have access to cooking facilities at your school, the potluck is your best bet. If you do have access (at FCHS we have three stoves and a fridge available), some of the following cooking options would work well, too.

The Good Food Class Meal (Keeping It Simple)—Rotini with Pesto, Tomatoes, and Cheese

This was the first class meal we ever held. We looked first at what we had in the garden: a lot of basil and tomatoes. Joe and I made a lot of pesto, chopped tomatoes, and then gave everyone a bowl. We set up a pasta serving line and shared our small bowls of pasta together. This was a simple and delicious first class meal.

A simple meal with help from our school garden.

The Good Food Class Meal—Burritos

Joe and I based our definition of good food on what we had in our school garden. We roasted butternut squash, slowly cooked down black beans, roasted tomatoes, made fresh pico de gallo and lemon cabbage. Joe also made baba ghanoush, and I pickled some red onions. For kicks we also made a hot sauce out of some jalapeños. Then we set up a burrito line and filled our plates.

The Good Food Class Meal—Burritos (the Class Cooks Together)

For this meal, we compiled a grocery list a couple of weeks in advance because we knew we were going to need large supplies of ingredients. We showed the list to our students, and each class claimed an item(s) on the list to bring to school on the cooking day. Once we had all the

Treasure making her burrito.

ingredients, each of our four classes took a section of the meal. One class made beans and rice. One class cut and roasted vegetables. One class made pico de gallo and lemon cabbage. One class made roasted tomato sauce and hot sauce. We cooked large amounts of each item, which were enough for all the classes for the next day.

Red cabbage for a class meal slaw.

Practicing knife skills in prep for a class meal.

Recipe for Organizing a Class Meal: What the Class Does

Here is a sample of what happens during the beginning, middle, and end of class meal as a way to organize the class. (This is for a seventy-minute class.) Even though the type of class meal will change throughout the year, giving a meal a beginning, middle, and end stays the same.

Appetizer—When students arrive, they put their bags away in one part of the room. Pens and small pads of paper are on the table (alternatively, students could write on the butcher paper tablecloth), and students do a quickwrite to start. The prompt: What is a meal? Write your definition. Or, How is your dish good food? (We respond to this or another prompt while we are doing last-minute things like uncovering dishes and making sure our bags are in one place in the room, out of the way.)

Main Course—We do two class shares, the quicker the better: (1) share your dish—what you brought and who it connects to and what's in it; (2) give a word of thanks; go around the room for a simple word (or more) from everyone.

Then, let's eat!

Dessert—Class slide show and/or go outside, if possible. You could also do a quick class cleanup, table games, a family (class) portrait, a reflection on a butcher paper tablecloth, etc.

English, Enchiladas, and Home: When Home Comes to School via a Class Meal (Jennifer S.)

When I started out my sophomore year at Fern Creek I was mystified to see a class named Food Lit on my schedule. I was like "What's Food Lit?" I found out that it was an English class, although not your ordinary idea of one. Food Lit, as I came to find out, is a class involving the connection between literature, culture, and yes, food. Students are taught the importance of not only defining a main theme in a piece of literature or main idea of an article, but also the ideas behind the making of said piece. Mr. Peters and Mr. Franzen taught us to extend our minds to the background that makes the appearance of either literature, food, or moral ideas. They did this by exploring different cultural backgrounds, and, by looking at a certain culture, we discovered the ideas of the culture itself and the influence that these ideas have on their traditions such as their meals.

Being the daughter of two Hispanic parents I found myself entertained by the discovery of these various cultures. I often reflected back to my mother's own cooking and came up with the idea to bring her in to make a meal for the class. One of my favorite meals is red enchiladas with flavored rice. When I spoke to my mother she was more than happy to come in to share a piece of our culture. As she always says nowadays: in order to help others accept our Hispanic community, we have to share our culture with them.

Hispanics have been criticized for a long time and blamed for problems that America faces constantly. We are downsized for being mostly poor and having to work really hard for everything we need including food and shelter. My family is no exception. What others don't realize is the strength that comes with our people in order to cross the physical and emotional barriers that are set upon us. Hispanics, particularly Mexicans, are built on the belief to always give your best no matter what you face. Boys are taught from a young age that in order to get through life you need to physically work hard, this being the reason that many of these young men start working in fields and construction at the age of 12, sometimes younger. Girls are taught from the age of 10 to keep everything neat and organized—thus they are taught to cook, clean, and wash. Mexicans know the virtue of honesty and responsibility, and it is why we are such a proud people.

My mother told me her story, much like the examples above, as she was preparing the enchiladas and rice for my class. She told me how at the age of eight she was in charge of her younger brother all while having the responsibilities of cooking, cleaning, doing laundry, and going to school. I've always known she was strong-willed but that was when I really saw her true strength. While making the enchiladas she frequently burned herself from the oil that was being used yet somehow she never complained. When making enchiladas, oil is used to soften the corn tortillas and give them an exceptional taste. My mother would dip the tortillas on both sides all while the oil burned her hands when it sizzled. Next came the rice. In order to soften the rice, it needs to be in boiling water and my mother came in contact with that water

Jennifer S. with her mom.

quite a bit. But I saw her pride in the way she kept cooking and admired her for staying strong just to help involve my peers in our ways.

Once the class meal was done, I looked in my mother's eyes and saw the joy from watching my classmates gratefully eat her food. Now every time we eat enchiladas at home I notice that same happiness displayed across my mother's face and have discovered that many other Hispanic mothers go through the same feeling with their families. This class meal and several others enjoyed throughout my year in Food Lit will stay with me forever. It's because of these class meals that I have learned to really look at the world in a different perspective. I now see the ideas behind various people, literature, and even countries as I look through articles in newspapers of global events and analyze them for not just the words in the article but also the ideas that come with them.

Voice + Home: A Parent's Perspective (Sherry S.)

Food Lit sounded like a really fun class for my son Noah when he was a sophomore at Fern Creek High School. Little did we know what an impact these teachers and this class would have on our family, and Noah's friends.

English was not Noah's favorite subject, but food was a whole different story. Mr. Franzen and Mr. Peters were showing the kids how to enjoy English through food. They were learning how to farm and how to take those ingredients and make beautiful food while writing about it. They had a garden, and live chickens. Some of them had never even seen a live chicken and now they were feeding them, caring for them, and even selling the eggs. My son LOVED this class.

Sherry S. and son, Noah, at class meal.

Honestly I had never met two teachers with so much passion about teaching kids and helping them see our great big world with new eyes.

The kids decided that some of the other employees in the school needed to reap the benefits of them learning to cook. We wanted them to know how it felt to spoil and serve others. The students decided they wanted to show their appreciation for the janitors and cafeteria workers. They decided to serve them by cooking them a Christmas dinner.

With the help of Franzen and Peters, the kids cooked the whole meal. They made baked spaghetti, salad, homemade dressing, bread, and even decorated gingerbread houses for the tables. The dinner was a huge success and the kids could not wait to do this every year.

Noah's Dad was diagnosed with terminal cancer in 2013, and I believe with all my heart that Noah's life was made easier by the love and support that he got from the teachers and students in this class. They were more than just teachers; they were Noah's support at school. They had all become closer through the bond of what they were learning in this class. They loved on my boy through food and English—imagine that. In the coming years all of the kids became more comfortable around the kitchen.

Noah and friends learned how to make bread and sold it to the teachers. They eventually had to shut down the baking as they could not keep up with the demand. Haha! I could go on and on about this class and all of the life lessons that the students and the parents learned.

It teaches how to care for ourselves and others with what the earth gives us and then lets the kids learn how fun writing about something can be once you have invested your time in it. It gave the kids confidence, and showed them something that they will be able to take with them when they leave high school.

I am a firm believer that food brings people together and Food Lit and Food Studies at Fern Creek is showing that every day in the life of our kids!!

Whole Wheat Bread Recipe (Sherry S.)

◎   ◎   ◎   ◎

6 C milled flour = 2 loaves
I like to use 5 cups of wheat flour and 1 cup of white flour, but you don't have to do this. I just think it makes it more moist.

Mix one package of dry yeast, ½ cup water at 110 degrees, and a spoonful of sugar in a small bowl. Let sit.

In Mixing Bowl stir:
1¾ C lukewarm water
¼ C olive oil
⅓ C honey

Mix with yeast mixture.
Add 3 cups flour to yeast mixture.
Once bubbly and doubled, add 2½ tsp salt.

Gradually add last 3 cups of flour.
Knead on 1 or 2 speed for 12 minutes; when done it should be like taffy and won't rip.

Pat dough into a large smooth ball and cover with moist towel. Let rise 1½ hours in warm place. Done rising when poke with finger and it barely moves.
Press down.
Pull out mush into a circle and cut in half. Roll out and then pull the dough like a diaper; cover on counter and rest 10 minutes while oiling your bread pans with softened butter.

Put in pans and rise another 30–40 minutes again.

350°F oven for 30 minutes.

When bread comes out, it should have an internal temperature of 190°F.

Try not to eat the whole loaf before your family gets home!!

Questions to Chew On

1. How can I bring home and school together in my classroom and school throughout the year?

2. How can I expand my understanding of students' backgrounds in my classroom?

3. What invitations could I make to help students connect with their identities, histories, and cultures?

4. What role does community play in my classroom? How can I sustain and build on the strong community I already have?

5. What can I celebrate in my class that will bring my group together as a community? How does that celebration look different at various times in the year?

A School Garden (and Outside) as a Classroom

Our first class meal establishes community, trust, and an ability to be open to and count on one another—and to follow where our learning leads us. The class meal is an opportunity to build on these things and generate other invitations. One of the strongest invitations is to our school garden, where we can explore, connect with where food comes from, and think about the garden as a classroom space that offers life, nourishment, curiosity, and a sensory experience. A lot of kids know we have a garden at school, but they may not have been in it. For some, the garden is a place where they feel at home and want to spend more time (Joe will explain this strong connection later). My knowledge of how the garden works is limited (but growing), but I use time in the garden as a way to grow my own knowledge and to invite kids to join a colleague's Garden Club or another colleague's Environmental Science class so that they can be in the garden and in the outdoors more.

If you don't have a garden at your school, you could start a small garden in some pots, in barrels, or in a small raised bed, or you could simply take your students for a walk outside. What follows is a lesson that is part of our Seeds and Gardens unit called Garden Wisdom. We go to the garden to observe, think, and write. The most important element of inviting the class to be outside and open to seeing and thinking about new things is that I'm taking the step as a teacher toward what David Sobel calls a "place-based pedagogy," one that encourages kids to learn to "make a difference in the here and now" by connecting to the story of the land around the school in addition to places throughout the school building (*Place-Based Education* 18). What I also want to accomplish by taking kids outside is to clearly communicate that this class will sometimes go outside, starting here and building up to Campfire, which is our literature circle and food and text pairing activity. We also go outside throughout the year to read, to write, and to work as peer editors. By going outside, we open up the many possibilities of using our whole school as a classroom.

Spending time in the garden as a classroom also opens up the world—to seeing how our place connects us to other places that are close or far away, and to seeing how viewing and reading food production in our place puts us in conversation with family stories and stories from around the world. Food can become a way of connecting to, caring about, and understanding the complexities and paradoxes of the world around us. The following strategy, Garden Wisdom, attempts to connect us to our local place while also inviting us to reach beyond our place to other cultures, worldviews, and time periods.

Garden Wisdom: Water-Soaked Philosophers

Bread feeds the body, indeed, but flowers feed also the soul.

—*The Koran*

All gardening is landscape painting.

—*William Kent*

As part of our Seeds and Gardens unit lesson, we choose two quotes from a large list of texts related to gardens by philosophers, artists, authors, and scientists from across the world and across time. We prod at the quotes word by word, questioning, affirming, pushing back, stumbling upon things, making personal connections, linking the quotes to what is happening in the world, changing the quotes into a question or into their antitheses. We call this strategy Blowing UP! a quote. This close reading encourages annotation, re-reading, and the discovery of rooms in our minds where new thoughts can go.

We find that a short, impactful, and enduring quote is much like a great work of literature. Our aim is to acknowledge the ways that words are powerful, and the multiple ways that a single sentence can be boundless in literal and figurative meaning. To "unlock" the potential wisdom of these quotes, we take a walk—markers and papers in hand—to our school garden in search of additional meaning and context, and to enjoy being in the garden and soaking in its wisdom, too.

"Walk around, discover, let your quotes move through your mind while you do. Explore and get close to what interests you. Eventually find a Leopold bench, a pallet chair, a picnic table, a raised-bed bench, and go back to your quote. Try to see your quote in a new light . . . with new eyes." Then I start to feel a few droplets of rain.

"Mr. Peters, it looks like it's going to rain. Should we go back in?"

"We can. Do you all think we should go in? Or just wait and see what the weather does?"

"We should stay out here. It won't take long to go back in if we need to."

Finding wisdom in chicken coops.

Then we scatter. Some groups head immediately to the greenhouse as this fine mist begins to cool what had been an unseasonably warm October day. Others go solo or as pairs to find "their" place. Some go straight to the chicken coop, some to the student-built pavilion; others work at large wooden cable-wire spools, gathered and repurposed by students into tables during our school's remodel. I walk around to check in with everyone—to ask questions, to observe, to encourage students to consider their quote from a plant's perspective, an older person's perspective, or from a child's or an artist's perspective, to see how their quotes hold up.

Olivia flags me down from the opposite side of the garden. She has a particularly dejected look on her face, a clear sign of thought roadblock. Her quote is from *The Koran*: "Bread feeds the body, indeed, but flowers feed also the soul."

"Mr. Peters, I'm not sure what this quote means; I think I need to start over with another one."

I read and re-read the quote. I know my thinking process is under observation, and I'm giving the quote the thought, care, and frustration that I know Olivia has already given it. I'm

Olivia and her quote in the FCHS garden.

also grappling with how to find a way into the quote for Olivia. I ask Olivia to try to separate the ideas in the quote. "'Bread feeds the body'; what do you think about when you read that?"

"I get that, Mr. Peters, like when you're hungry. Bread can feed the body, that's physical hunger. But is this quote trying to say that we should eat flowers?"

"Maybe, but maybe we shouldn't eat them in the same way that we eat bread. Is there some other way we could "eat" flowers? Is there some other way that people are hungry? How can flowers feed people besides physical hunger?"

"Well, flowers are beautiful. I suppose we need beauty in our lives."

"Ok. Let's follow that idea. . . ."

I look around Olivia and see and smell a garden bed perfuming our conversation with the scent of marigolds. I pick two: one with a deep red and bright gold bloom, one with a drooping, drying, fading bloom.

We smell the marigold in full bloom. Olivia tells me that flowers make her think of funerals, Valentine's Day, and spring, that flowers carry a lot of associations, some sad and some joyous. Then we look at the dried up, dying flower. I pull at the dry petals and show Olivia all the seeds inside the stem that the plant is getting ready to let go of to become other marigolds. She puts the seeds on top of her quote—creating an entirely new dimension to annotation on the spot, a living annotation—leading her to a new thought that brings the words on the page to life as well.

"So even after this flower dies, there's a part of it that goes on living, that goes on becoming flowers."

"Yes, it seems that way." And I begin to notice that the rain is picking up a bit. In my survey of all the garden retreats, I see that the rain isn't causing anyone to stir, in spite of our lack of preparation.

"So maybe this quote is about how flowers feed a deeper part of us, and I guess that's our soul, Mr. Peters."

"What is a soul, Olivia?"

"Well, I've heard it said that it's like the part of us that never dies. It goes on living even after we are gone. Maybe flowers teach us about how we live on, and that is what this quote means. That this flower's life can make all these little flowers live on, too." Then she points to all the marigold seeds on her paper.

"Olivia, I never would have seen this quote so clearly without hearing you say what you just said."

Alexis and Olivia in the garden (before the rain).

I look up at a sign on the raised bed next to Olivia, and I'm even more astonished. It says, *Suk Man, In Remembrance.* The rain is picking up even more, but still no stirring. I ask Olivia to look up at the sign that students made for Suk, a Nepali student who died in a car accident the previous year. Fern Creek students planted this raised bed and some pawpaw trees on our campus to celebrate Suk's life and to preserve his memory. Olivia continues.

"This raised bed is more than the plants in it; it's more like the flower in the quote—a space to feed the soul and a way to live on. Now it makes sense that this quote is from the Koran, which is a holy book. This quote is about feeding our spiritual hunger."

I understand the quote for the first time, too, and I also understand that the rain has become a near downpour, we're all getting soaked, but no one is in a hurry to leave, even though we're at the point where puddle jumping seems like a good idea.

When we get back to the room, we hold up our papers, which look like they've gone through the washing machine. Kids ask jokingly where I want them to turn their papers in, if they should hang them up to dry, and if they should go tell the next class they're going outside today, too. We are giddy. Most of our annotations have washed away . . . but something much more important has remained.

I look down at my garden quote from William Kent: "All gardening is landscape painting." I really pushed back against this quote when we were in the classroom, when I was modeling how to Blow UP! a quote. I pushed back because I thought it reduced the garden, confined it. Now my notes around the quote are orange and purple ink smears that look oddly floral, and I realize how a garden *can* be a watercolor landscape painting—and how the landscape that a garden can paint is us. We went out to the garden as a class and came back newly painted and water-soaked philosophers, with a shared experience and memory that is inside us to stay.

Garden Wisdom: A Recipe

1. Choose two quotes from a list of quotes about gardens (or any other topic).
2. Write the quotes (one to each side) on a piece of construction paper.
3. Walk around the garden. Smell, taste, touch, listen, watch. What is interesting to you? What do you see? (Try to see the garden from different levels, too.)
4. Find a place in the garden to sit and think. Soak things in, and think about your quotes in relation to being in the garden.
5. Annotate/Blow UP! the quotes—write around the quotes, circling words in the quotes, too. Write about:
   - specific words (diction) and their literal and figurative meanings
   - questions you have about the quote
   - how the quote relates to big ideas or the world
   - whether you agree with or take issue with the quote
   - how the quote relates to people, to you, to our school garden, etc.

Note: We have done this activity substituting various topics that coincide with thematic units to include quotes about love, compassion, water, money, etc.

Campfire: Food and Text Pairings

Campfire Introduction: What It Is and What It Does

Campfire is our Food Lit literary analysis circle around a food pairing that happens inside and outside the classroom throughout the year, depending on the weather. Sometimes the food and text pairing is a literal one, as in the case of cake and the short essay "Dessert" by Colum McCann (see below), and other times the pairing is more figurative or requires an imaginative leap, as in the case of the poem "Abandoned Farmhouse" by Ted Kooser and fresh baked bread and jam. The food pairing provides a way back into a text through the sensory overlap of the food item juxtaposed with the text and the students' critical, creative, and analytical connections I invite them to make between the two texts, bringing our group and our discussion to life. The passage we use for Campfire is usually a short piece that students are seeing for the first time. This is important because by reading a new text we are helping one another gain confidence with new texts and modeling reading strategies such as re-reading, annotation, questioning, and inferencing, as well as speaking and listening strategies. What we annotate a text for changes depending on the skill we are working on in class. In discussion, I prompt the kids to focus on the one thing in the text—the one word, one question, one device, one connection, one sentence, etc.—that they think no one else sees. This tunes up our eyes for discovery and takes us beyond the surface level of the text. In short, our group grapples with a text together so that we will eventually be better at grappling with new texts on our own. By the end of Campfire, we will have heard every voice, and we will also have heard what is music to English teachers' ears—the sound of kids building on one another's ideas and naming each other in the process. By extension, what starts to emerge is an understanding that we can support each other through our learning by all of us becoming teachers who allow others to see new things. This establishes what Paulo Freire calls a "humanizing pedagogy," in which the teacher and the students are "both simultaneously teachers *and* students" (53).

Here are the steps to Campfire that we follow with any food and text pairing. We post these steps next to the circle each time we hold Campfire:

1. **Read the passage aloud.**

2. **Read the passage again (to yourself, silently) and annotate for the focus skill (i.e., literary devices, diction, characterization, tone shifts, etc.).**

3. **Share one thing with the class that will make us all think.** (Each student has about forty-five seconds to share while the group listens closely, adds to their annotations, and snaps after each classmate shares or gets them thinking.)

4. **Food pairing + think:** I introduce a food item, we enjoy the food item together, with freedom to move about and talk, and I challenge students to think about how the food item relates to the text.

5. **Write.** (We bring the group back together and everyone writes for five minutes about their specific, unique connection between the food item and the text.)

6. **Share.** (We hear from as many as time permits.)

7. **Yum!** (We walk away fed with new ideas, thoughts, and questions.)

What follow are two takes on Campfire. The first pairing, which I've titled "My Food Lit Class That Smells like Corn," helps answer why we do Campfire, and the second pairing, "A Piece of Cake after 9/11," takes you inside the Campfire circle discussion to see where the connections to food and literature can go.

My Food Lit Class That Smells like Corn: How Campfire Changes a Classroom

Literary Text: "My Lucy Friend Who Smells like Corn" (from *Woman Hollering Creek* by Sandra Cisneros)

Food Text: Corn Pudding

As an English teacher, I understand that stories and food have the ability to take us home. When we bring the two together—especially for English language learners—the classroom is a welcome mat for bringing home, experience, developing language skills, and stories to the table.

My kids speak "food," "story," and "home" together at our Food Lit Campfire.

Campfire is foremost a strategy to highlight the magic of a writer and a literary text with the addition of a food that relates to the text. We read the text first and choose one line, one word, or one question. We write about our "one thing" and then share it with the group. Then we add a layer of understanding by reading the text and the food item together to take a bite out of literature and memory.

Our passage is Sandra Cisneros's "My Lucy Friend Who Smells like Corn" from *Woman Hollering Creek.* Cisneros's piece seems to be challenging us to fill the room with the smell of corn, and we do! I bring in homemade corn pudding—the recipe that my wife, Emily, used to serve at her café—and I reheat a batch before each class so that the scent goes out the door and into the hallway, leading my kids (and lots of other kids) into the room. When the students arrive, they see a table filled with individual plates of corn pudding next to Cisneros's text. They know today is Campfire.

In "My Lucy Friend," the young narrator tells her story using mostly English and some Spanish words. The pace of her words is excited and quick. She praises and adores her Lucy like a sister, and she is as fond of the smell of corn on Lucy as she is of all the memories and adventures that she and Lucy have together. The narrator's English usage shows that she is learning English, and kids are quick to notice what Cisneros is communicating through her use of syntax—that the story is more important than every word or sentence being perfectly correct. This opens up discussions about the meanings and connotations of English and Spanish words, and conversations about the smell and significance of corn from tortillas versus corn from corn pudding. My students tell me that to get closer to the text and the smell of corn that Cisneros is talking about we could make tortillas. And next time we will—together.

In our discussion, we connect the story, the food text, the recipe, the corn pudding's link to the story, and all our stories around corn and the smell of corn. As well, we ask some of the questions that take us beneath the surface of the text and our own experiences: *Why does Lucy smell like corn? Why does the narrator concentrate so much on Lucy and so little on herself? What does **your** childhood smell and taste like, and why?* We discover that we have companion smells and tastes to match Lucy's smell of corn. As we give voice to these stories, we discover what possibly motivated Cisneros to write this story in the first place. We learn what our stories and our English sound like too, and what our stories have to teach us about language, home, memory, and the overlap between them.

Our stories take us beyond our homes in Louisville. We explore other parts of the United States that we call home; other countries such as Bosnia, Nepal, China, Cambodia, and Mexico where our families came from; and the childhood homes of our parents and grandparents that we know through story. We share these stories while the scent of corn pudding lingers in the air.

We are all learning English, and Campfire shows us how learning English means learning new words and stories, reading closely, listening to each other, writing and speaking our words and thoughts, and learning how to value one another as teachers of English. Our Food Lit classroom smells like corn sometimes, like our class meal at other times, like applesauce, like tea, and as much as possible—like home.

EMILY'S CORN PUDDING RECIPE FOR PAIRING WITH "MY LUCY FRIEND WHO SMELLS LIKE CORN"

This is a recipe that my wife, Emily, used to serve at her café in Louisville called the Butterfly Garden Café. She made this corn pudding every morning, and it's the perfect complement to "My Lucy Friend" because it's my way of bringing home and story to the class, as well as a delicious way to fill the room with the scent of corn. For any food pairing, you can either make or buy the item. The "Lucy Friend" piece, for example, would work just as well with popcorn or tortilla chips. If you can, invite kids to stay and cook the day before Campfire because it creates the sense of the class giving back to and helping to create the class, which is such a nice dynamic. I don't always have time to do this, and my kids definitely remind me when I don't.

◎　◎　◎　◎

Corn Pudding
Makes 12–16 pieces

1 large onion, diced
2 Tbsp butter
2 Tbsp milk
2 large eggs
2 (8½ oz) boxes yellow corn muffin mix
1 (14¼ oz) can cream-style corn
1 (4 oz) can diced green chilies, drained
¼ C chopped pimentos
⅓ C sour cream
1 C shredded sharp cheddar cheese, optional

Preheat oven to 425 degrees. Grease 9" × 13" baking pan.

Melt the butter in a small pan over medium high heat. Add the onion and cook until translucent, about 5 minutes. Remove from heat and set aside.

In a medium bowl, stir together milk, eggs, corn bread mix, creamed corn, chilis, and pimentos. Pour the corn bread mixture into the greased pan.

Spoon the sauteed onions and sour cream into the corn bread mixture and swirl throughout, as if you were making a marble cake. Top with cheese, if desired.

Bake 30–40 minutes. Let the corn pudding cool for 10 minutes or more before cutting. Serve warm or at room temperature.

Refrigerate for up to one week or freeze for up to 6 months. Reheat the entire pan at 350° for 20 minutes or in pieces in the microwave.

◎　◎　◎　◎

A Piece of Cake after 9/11

Still there is a need, now and always, for sharply felt local intimacies.

—Colum McCann

Literary Text: "Dessert" by Colum McCann

Food Text: Chocolate Cake

In Colum McCann's piece "Dessert," from the *New Yorker* on the tenth anniversary of 9/11, the narrator encounters a lady eating a piece of chocolate cake the day after the Twin Towers fell. The narrator has no idea what to make of the woman and eventually says that he doesn't know whether to be upset at the woman and the way she ate the cake or whether "it was one of the most audacious acts of grief" he's ever seen. We took this wonderful piece of McCann's to our Campfire to try to figure out our answer.

Though my generation can recount clearly exactly where we were on 9/11, my group of sophomores were born after 2001. While they know of the events of 9/11, they don't carry the impact of that day in the same way an older generation does. But McCann's piece provides intensity and suspicion, and encapsulates how uncertainty mixed with emotion made people doubt their notions of what could be considered "normal." The narrator in McCann's piece is attempting to understand whether he can trust the motivation behind the woman's "audacious" act of eating a piece of cake . . . alone.

In our Food Lit Campfire, we are all invited to grapple along with the narrator. We circle the benches under a large oak tree next to our school garden. The acorns that drop from the tree on this September day become a startling accompanying text that helps us to read the uncertainty and the random shout of small and large collisions in the text. As a backdrop, the rooster in our school garden calls out again and again, reminding us that this is our September 12, in conversation with McCann's September 12. To add a layer to our experience, we pair McCann's essay with cake that our Cooking Club made the day before so that we can have cake with the woman in McCann's piece.

While the class reads and annotates the text, Joe and I move from student to student to see how the process is going. When we are finished annotating, we place a cake, uniced, on the bench in the middle of the Campfire circle and bring ingredients out of a cooler—butter, powdered sugar, a bit of milk, vanilla, and some Hershey's cocoa—for buttercream icing. We show the kids how to make the icing, and they can't believe how easy it is (and how much sugar is in icing). Then we ice the cake in front of them while they're writing down a thought about the text to share with the group.

In Campfire circle, we are trying to create an intimate and invitational space where we can connect a number of texts—McCann's text, the cake, ourselves, and the outdoors. Then a plane flies overhead. We couldn't have planned this if we had tried.

Food and text pairing for Campfire.

Buttercream Icing
1½ C butter (3 sticks), softened
1 C unsweetened cocoa
4 C confectioner's sugar
½ C milk
1 tsp vanilla extract

The goal of Campfire is to prove just how rich our reading of a text becomes when we carefully consider how others read and respond to the text. We invite everyone to share the one thing that resonates with them—the one thought, question, device, word, or string of words that only they see. Then we move around the circle and share this thought, adding to our annotations as we go. Round one of Campfire is a reading of the text only.

Then we cut the cake and give each student a piece. The group waits until everyone has been served before they dig in. The second round of Campfire always includes a food pairing like this. The kids are used to this structure, and they know that we aren't simply eating cake today; we are reading cake in a way that will help us to enter the text in a new way.

"Can we eat it?"

"Of course you can, but when you do, think about how you can read this cake and all that's connected to it—the ingredients, the preparation, the plate, and the way that your thoughts about cake takes you back to McCann's text. Go deep, and think about the literal and the figurative here. Make us really think."

Some gulp the cake down and then ask for milk. (We do have a little milk on hand . . . a personal weakness too.) Others are more deliberate and Zen-like; they try to eat the cake like the woman in the text, slowly and with a seeming mindlessness. They are thinking and jotting down some thoughts. I'm also excited to see smiles, laughter, informal conversations, and even play, and give students time for this as well. As I look around the circle, I see a class celebrating, attending to one another while they are experiencing many texts at once.

We bring the conversation back in to the whole group. New texts are now in front of most of us and inside of us—an empty plate with crumbs around our forks and the aftertaste of cake. We are much like the woman in the story and much like the narrator viewing the woman in the story. I now realize that the invitation to "read" cake is an invitation to read the entire dynamic process of the cake—from the baking to the consumption and now to the remains—and that reading food provides layers upon layers that are not lost on our kids.

Campfire in session under a shade oak.

They read the cake, the plate, the fork, the crumbs, and themselves. One student jumps in to start a pulsating wave of discussion.

"What McCann is doing here is undoing the positive associations that we have with layer cake. We normally think of cake in relation to parties and celebrations. After 9/11, even the symbols of joy are not joyful. Things have been turned upside down like the fork on the plate."

"I think the lady is a symbol of strength. She's keeping her appointment the day after 9/11, being there even though the person she would be meeting won't be there. Maybe that person she's waiting for was lost in the Twin Towers. As I was eating the cake, I thought about how the cake was shaped like the Twin Towers, and how all the language of destruction in the passage somehow suggests how she's somewhat ashamed that her attempt to connect with someone via the cake only puts her closer to the tragedy of the towers."

"The lady and the narrator are facing what should be a familiar view—a person eating in a café—only the view to them isn't familiar anymore because a part of their world is gone; a part of themselves is gone too. Their world looks different to them than it did the day before."

"Maybe the piece is really about the regret that is in the narrator but can't be spoken, kind of like the unspoken conversation between the woman and the narrator. Instead of talking to the woman, the speaker is suspicious of her. There's a lot of irony here because when the buildings were knocked down, this piece shows that the result was the strengthening of the protective walls between people. The speaker isn't able to knock down a wall and be there for the woman, but I understand why he doesn't say something to her. I don't think I would be able to talk to her either."

Then someone raises a hand and says, "Mr. Peters, Mr. Franzen, you ruined cake for me. I'm never going to be able to eat cake again without thinking about this. Thanks a lot!" This gets a lot of laughs, and a half-hearted apology with a question mark at the end of it from both of us. Then another student jumps in.

"I think about what you said about not being able to forget, right. Well, this piece wasn't written on 9/12/01. It was written on the ten-year anniversary of 9/11, on 9/11/11. I think about what you said in a new way now, that somehow the writing of this piece was a way for the writer/speaker to break down a wall and to become acquainted with the woman again; he carried the memory of her for ten years. The speaker is in some way letting go and moving on, like the lady was able to do after she ate the cake. The speaker has just taken a lot longer to finish his cake."

We have this entire discussion with icing still on our hands and faces. When the response papers are turned in, they stick to each other and have small circular butter cream patches that make the papers translucent when held up to the light. When I'm looking over the responses after school, I see how one text has indeed "become" another in Campfire, how very literally the text will be walking around inside of us for a while, too, and how a text about distance, isolation, unspoken grief, and longing to understand has created the possibility for a class born before September 11, 2001, to get close to the heart of the emotions of that day. McCann's writing created this intimacy, but through Campfire I see how experiencing literature together is helping our group gain confidence as readers and confidence in their ability to make connections within and beyond a literary text—and to see how the most poignant texts can read us, too.

Some Additional Food Lit Campfire Pairings

"The Open Boat" by Stephen Crane and miso soup

Pablo Neruda's odes and tomatoes, lemons, apples, onions, etc.

"I Love the Look of Words" by Maya Angelou and popcorn

"The Bear" by Anton Chekhov and gummy bears

Chapter 6 from *The Glass Castle* by Jeannette Walls and Mounds and Three Musketeers bars

"Abandoned Farmhouse" by Ted Kooser and bread with jam

Chapter 15 from *The Grapes of Wrath* by John Steinbeck and peppermint candy

A Raisin in the Sun by Lorraine Hansberry and grapes, raisins, raisin bread, and scrambled eggs

"The Distance of the Moon" by Italo Calvino and moon milk (your imagined recipe)

Chapter 1 from *The Bluest Eye* by Toni Morrison and milk

"A Case for Eating Dog" (from *Eating Animals*) by Jonathan Safran Foer and beef jerky

Excerpts from *Charlie and the Chocolate Factory* by Roald Dahl and chocolate

Chapter 5 from *Salt Sugar Fat* by Michael Moss and Coca-Cola

"The Bean Eaters" by Gwendolyn Brooks and black bean salsa with chips

Excerpts from *Andy Catlett: Early Travels* by Wendell Berry and raspberry hand pies

William Shakespeare's *Othello* and strawberry shortcake

Chapter 5 from *The Great Gatsby* by F. Scott Fitzgerald and lemon cake and tea

The Kite Runner by Khaled Hosseini and a recipe from *Food Path: Cuisine along the Grand Trunk Road* by Pushpesh Pant

Excerpts from *The Dorito Effect* by Mark Schatzker and Doritos

The Curiosity + Challenge Project: The Homework We've Always Wished For

One of the most common answers we get from kids when we ask, "How was your winter break?" in January is, "Boring."

We had to try to do something about this, so for our Food Lit class Joe and I created the Curiosity + Challenge Project. Curiosity + Challenge is permission to take on something you have always wanted to do. Think of it as the homework you always wished you could have.

As a teacher, I think about what I communicate before a break—and how important that communication is for kids. Do I let the class come to a stopping point and then start again after two weeks, or do I create a bridge between the first and second semesters? I have let the class stop and start by giving a test or making a larger paper due; I have given kids various reading projects that brought mixed results; and I have started the new term with brand-new content. These approaches didn't always communicate care, or even acknowledge that we and the kids were having a break that would include some of the most important components to great learning—time, family, food, and gifts. In other words, we were about ready to experience a time of the year when we could all ask our family members for things (like a sketchbook, a guitar, a camera, etc.) and they would potentially get those things for us. We also had time to help family, do service, ask our grandparents questions, or soak in family stories. We would all be doing a lot, thinking a lot, and making new discoveries. Joe and I would be doing all these things over the break, too. We had to connect all these things and, more important, create an avenue by which to bring these things back to class with us. The Curiosity + Challenge Project helps us to do all of this while simultaneously helping the class grow closer.

The project is simple: make a list of all the things you are curious about next to a list of challenges you have always had for yourself, and then look at these two lists side by side. A few items will stand out—things that are more doable or more interesting to you than the others on the list. With the ones that stand out most, we make what we call a Curiosity + Challenge Equation, wherein we create our challenge project by either turning a curiosity into a challenge, or by starting in on a challenge we have always had for ourselves. We then choose the equation that we most want to focus on and write our final challenge equation with a bold marker on a sheet of paper. We create these challenge equations about three days before the break. When we share our initial equations, the room is full of excitement and possibility—kids are ready to get started on their projects.

The next step in the process is to set ourselves up for success by finding support from home, from our community, and from class. We call or text home to get permission to do the project. Some of the projects might change after this, and sometimes someone from home will become a part of the project. Regardless, this check-in makes the project real and communicates to parents that the project is being planned out and will be a part of the winter break. We also call other family members who might be able to help. If a project requires making a connection in the community, we make those calls during class before the break starts. Kids might call various organizations to see about volunteering, for instance. Then we make connections in the school with other teachers who may be able to help us with our projects. Students talk to those teachers before their break starts to line up information, talk through details, etc. Finally, kids select two peers they will check in on during their project and list two people to check in on them. Ideally, this creates accountability and encourages kids to network with one another, as well as inviting students to support each other and be supported by each other over the break. Once we have support in place, we make a quick checklist of things to do before getting started on the project—again, setting ourselves up for success.

When the students return from break, they all know to bring in their Curiosity + Challenge logs sheets and an artifact from their project to share with the rest of the class for our speed dating session, in which we share our projects with each other. Students may also schedule a day to present their projects more formally to the class. Some complete their projects over the break; others start their projects over the break and have a finish line much further away. Both cases work well. After the speed dating session, we write a more formal reflection and post a part of it on Schoology for others to see how our projects went, as well as to comment on them and view photos and videos that accompany the projects.

What I get out of these projects each year is the chance to learn more about my students and to discover the many ways we learn, including about ourselves. We find out a whole lot when we give ourselves the freedom to explore who we are and how we deal with a challenge. I have discovered that kids do more on their projects than I could ever have assigned them on any homework task. They research, problem-solve, network, and overcome challenges—in a supported way that is also on their own time schedule, all while having a lot of fun and learning not to be afraid of taking on something big that might not totally succeed. Long after we open our holiday gifts, we give ourselves the big gift of astonishing one another on the first day back from break by being able to reconsider what we thought we knew about others and ourselves. The result of these new discoveries about what makes us all work is that we are better able to acknowledge the same depth in all the texts we read and all the writing we do. Our class Curiosity + Challenge Equation = everything and everyone becomes more interesting!

Where Curiosity + Challenge Leads = Creative Writing Club and Empowerment (Trey H.)

Curiosity + Challenge has been among the most enriching and interesting projects I completed in high school, and honestly one of the few assignments that have influenced my life as a whole. Now, with my sappy admission out of the way, let's give a little explanation as to what it is.

Curiosity + Challenge is an odd project. It is given to all Food Literature students over winter break, which provides the students two weeks without school to work on whatever they want. That is the true secret behind the project, it is completely free form; all that is requested is a topic, or topics, of interest be chosen and some type of work be done with it. In my class, we had everything from someone calculating exactly how many generations it would take to get a certain type of Pokemon, to someone studying addiction and giving up caffeine, to my

Trey with his dad at a class meal.

own task of writing a short story. It's an opportunity to learn something that interests you without threat of reprisal, all Peters and Franzen want is to see the work you did. Bring in pictures to show the class, get up and explain your calculations and the process of farming Pokemon, read an excerpt. As long as you have something to share, you're golden.

Despite my sophomore laziness, I took the project seriously. My first step was to decide what to write, something new or a continuation of a story I had started that spring. The already begun piece (more akin to an outline than a story) won out, of course. After a week of middling work and much thought; I buckled down, grabbed some coffee, and promptly began reading other amateur short stories in an attempt to put off actually writing under the guise of "getting inspiration." It wasn't until 3 A.M. on the second Monday of break that I actually began writing. By the end of break I had a 29,000+ word short story and a passion I have yet to escape.

Of course, just writing a novella didn't spur me on to start the Creative Writing Club, or to become an English major. No, the presentation is what has kept me going. The week we all returned from winter break was almost entirely dedicated to presenting our projects, and I read the prelude (yes, I made a prelude to a novella) to the class. I stuttered and botched lines and was certain my classmates could hear my heartbeat the entire time; I was sure they would call it pedantic and silly; I was sure they didn't like it and all I had accomplished was embarrassing myself. I was wrong; one girl even said, "If you keep writing like that, you could make it as a writer." I wanted to write more and I wanted other people with that passion to feel how I felt. I wanted to give others praise and a reason to believe they had made something worth the hours of thinking, something they could be proud of. I wanted to share.

However, I was slow to act on this. The first meeting didn't take place until the end of April, 2014, and only two other meetings were held before school ended for the summer. That proved to be of little consequence; every Monday, we (Mr. Peters, Thomas T., Nicholas M., and myself) met at a Barnes and Noble to sit in their Starbucks and write. We weren't a large group, but we were dedicated. We made a framework for meetings, started stories, and grew closer over that summer.

Three years later, as a first-year in college, I can't help but wonder what I would be like had Curiosity + Challenge never been an option. What started as one teen who wanted to write grew into a group that published its own literary magazine in 2016 and that continues to function today. I wouldn't have started the club without that first project. I wouldn't have been confident enough to pick a liberal arts school or an English Major over computer science and UofL if I hadn't been given that one project. Through the freedom Food Literacy offered, students were given a voice. We were allowed to pursue what we wanted and develop what skills we valued. Creativity and freedom, two of the tenets of Food Literacy, allowed me to find my passion and help others find theirs.

Recipe: Curiosity + Challenge Equations

1. Fold a piece of paper in half (hot dog or hamburger). In one column, write "I am curious about," and on the other side write "I have always wanted to . . .".

2. List all the things you can think of in both of the columns, filling them in as much as you can. Then step back and look at the two columns. With an elbow partner, talk about some of the things on the list. Then think about what you might like to start over the break, and what you *could* start. Put a star by a few of the items that stand out.

3. On a strip of construction paper, attempt to write your Curiosity + Challenge Equation. It may take a few drafts. Share some of these with the class; the sharing will help those who are having some trouble. Also, share both your equation and your project plan.

4. Once you have the equation, create a simple checklist of things you need to get started on the project. Also, list two people who will be checking in on you during the project.

5. On the back of the equation, write the words "Finish Line," as well as when the project will be finished and what you will bring in to share with the class when we get back from break.

Curiosity + Challenge: Some Student Equations

I usually have students take a picture of their equations to keep for themselves, and then I hang all the equations up in the classroom so that we can all see what everyone is doing for their projects, which gives our class real momentum. Also, I have found that if I'm at school over the break, simply looking at the equations makes me so motivated and excited for our return to school. What I hope is that students are also looking forward to returning. They know what to expect when we get back from break, which resets the tone of the class and communicates clearly to kids that our class is about us and about taking on challenges that enable us to continually learn about ourselves and others, and to learn about how to learn through the process. Here are some of those equations:

Jordyn and Logan with their Curiosity + Challenge Equations.

Curiosity + Challenge = learning how to play a song on the piano all the way through and to document the process.
—Bailey C.

Curiosity + Challenge = begin blacksmithing
—Sebastian T.

Curiosity + Challenge = start learning parkour and start working out to build more muscle mass
—Ryan B.

Curiosity + Challenge = build the Empire State building out of legos
—Amar D.

Curiosity + Challenge = attempt to make the first two chapters of a full-length, full-sized comic book by the end of the break
—Donald B.

Curiosity + Challenge= a drawing a day
—Jenya M.

Curiosity + Challenge = 3D-print a bionic arm
—Mackenzie T.

Curiosity + Challenge = documenting the things/people that bring me happiness and become more aware of how important they are
—Grace C.

Curiosity + Challenge= learn how to make muffins and hopefully make some for Food Lit when they are good
—Malachi C.

Class Tea: The Basics

We usually have class tea in the winter months because having hot tea or cocoa is a great way to warm up on a cold day. We hold class teas a number of ways. Sometimes teas are more formal, like our Valentine's Day tea. Valentine's Day class tea works more like a class meal, where students sign up to bring small bites of food items like scones, cookies, dumplings, small sandwiches, etc. We also transform the classroom space into a Valentine's Day Café by decorating the room and the tables with our creative designs and our original poems. In addition, we compile our poetry into a Valentine's Day poetry anthology as a gift from the class to the class. Other times, class tea is more informal, as simple as having the basics set up on a table in the back of the room—hot water, tea bags, cream or milk, sugar, and spoons. We invite kids to bring in small tea snacks or cookies, but that's optional. During informal class teas, one section of the class might be devoted to reading, with kids reading while they drink tea or cocoa, or we might have tea on a day when we're sharing stories or poems we've written, or when we have visitors to the class as a way to be good hosts and to create a welcoming dinner table–like atmosphere. When kids enter the room and start making their tea or having a snack that a classmate has made and then shared, the action invites interaction and changes the pace of the day; it also makes us more at home together.

When you have a class tea, invite kids to explore the class's connection to a text that you may be reading in class or to the story of tea, its place of origin as well as its history. As far as taste, tea is an opportunity to try new flavors and experiment with various combinations and steeping methods, and we encourage this. If you don't have tea mugs, ask your kids to bring in a mug or teacup that represents them—you will be in for a pleasant surprise. Sometimes your tea aficionados will even bring in their own tea to share. Consider handing out a

Food Lit class tea setup.

scone (or other) recipe a couple of days before a class tea and see who might be interested in baking scones. I guarantee that recipe gets grabbed, taken home, and brought back in as delicious scones for everyone.

It is important to mention beforehand how setup and cleanup will work and for everyone to be safe and mindful of others around hot tea. You can either have students put hot water in their own cups, or you can bring hot water around in tea pots after your students have selected their teas. It is good to model how to steep tea and what to do with the tea bags once the tea has steeped. We usually place small bowls on the tables to collect the tea bags. Have some towels handy because there will be a few spills.

Have a tea with your class as well, and enjoy! The best part about your class tea is how you will make it your own!

Valentine's Day Class Tea: "Close-to-Perfect Acts of Love"

About two days before our last class tea, which was on Valentine's Day, Sasha came in with a bag filled with chocolate suckers in the shapes of hearts, kisses, and tiger claws. She asked me if I could hold on to them for class tea and that

I must make sure they didn't melt; they had to be refrigerated. "Promise me that you will put these in the refrigerator, Mr. Peters. I know how forgetful you are sometimes." She told me that her mom had stayed up until midnight the night before making these, and that today was her mom's birthday.

"I promise, Sasha."

I know many see Valentine's Day as an occasion to express exaggerated versions of love, but Sasha's mom's version was a real, valuable, and selfless act of love that motivated me and taught me what loving and compassionate acts can do. I wanted to be worthy of this act, and so set a goal for class tea to be as close to a perfect act of love as these chocolates were.

When I went to Kroger to do some shopping for the tea, I thought about how Sasha's mom had already done her shopping and devoted a lot of time and energy to our class in making the suckers. I felt humbled by her example. I filled up a shopping cart full of tea, coffee, cocoa, cups, plastic forks, paper plates, etc. I spent $60 or so on the tea—$60 I did not have to spend and had to explain when I got home. Our school and our Alumni Association

Sasha with her mom's famous chocolate suckers.

help so much with covering expenses, and I am incredibly grateful to them and for them, but sometimes I, like all teachers, chip in my own money.

Conventional wisdom says that teachers spend too much of their own money and time on their classrooms and that doing so can be counterproductive. I see some truth in this, but if I follow conventional wisdom today, we won't have a class tea tomorrow. I reach a point all the time in teaching where conventional wisdom and common sense say two different things—I always go with common sense. When I do, I understand that teachers aren't loners making sacrifices in our island classrooms. Instead, we are acting out shared and uncelebrated acts of nearly perfect love alongside parents, administrators, and students.

At the grocery store, I saw the proof of this on display. By scheduling a class tea, I had inadvertently set up an informal class meeting at the Fern Creek

Sasha and her mom, Beverly.

Kroger. While I was filling my shopping cart, I saw some of my students and their parents also shopping for class tea. I had a chance to meet a lot of parents for the first time and to thank them personally. We talked to each other and waved across aisles. I saw a shared desire to do something kind for all our kids, and that view from the grocery store inspired me in the same way that Sasha's bag of suckers did.

This grocery store view made me challenge the conventional route I travel to get to my classroom on any given day. Instead of the round trip to and from the copy room after school, I took a longer, meandering trip. First, I went to the Food Lab to get bowls, serving utensils, and a bag of sugar. I went to the ROTC room to borrow

Eileen, Olivia, and Emma on the morning of our Food Lit Valentine's Day class tea.

two large Gatorade coolers. I went to the main office to invite everyone to the tea the next day, and I went to the courtyard to cut flowers for place settings. Then I went to Kroger—again—for groceries, to Meijer for thank-you cards, and back to my room to see how the students had transformed the room while I was gone. This was not Room 137; this was a Valentine's Day Café. My kids didn't need this activity to be a special holiday; they were only waiting to be asked to contribute.

Those suckers definitely didn't melt; they made it intact to class the next day. They were wonderful. We had a joyous tea . . . thanks to shared attempts at close-to-perfect acts of love.

Panzenland, Our Food Lit Town: Some Background

The focus standards for our Food Lit class were about argumentation, and we had just finished a drama unit in which we staged the play *The Bear* by Anton Chekhov. Our kids did absolutely amazing on this, and they wanted more opportunities to be in front of their peers. We wanted our students to do research, to perform, and to develop complex arguments based on their study of a rhetorical situation and rhetorical appeals. When we devised the scenario for Panzenland, we didn't know how the scenario would work. Much like the class meal, we placed a lot of the responsibility for how the experience would play out on our students, the idea being that the more we all put in, the more we could get out of the experience and learn along the way. We discovered not only that the scenario worked, but also that it began to really matter to the kids, and going to the town meeting and eventually a town debate created a buzz and an energy that Joe and I could never have imagined. And we observed new aspects of our students start to surface, be expressed, and be embraced by others. While we were experiencing Panzenland, we were also working on more formal argumentative essays, and I know that the Panzenland experience enhanced the ways that our kids approached an argument, especially the ways they considered their audience, alongside the importance of addressing claims, counterclaims, concessions, and rebuttals.

We named our town Panzenland. Our kids named the town, and that name has stuck as the town has been passed down to subsequent classes. But the scenario is easily adaptable. What follows is a model for how you and your students can build a town and a scenario of your own.

The work of designing Panzenland draws on Viola Spolin's masterful *Improvisation for the Theater* in which she states that "healthy group expression demands a number of individuals working interdependently to complete a given project and with full individual participation and personal contribution" (9), which is the goal of Panzenland. We also credit the work of Eileen Landay and Kurt Wooten and their espousal of the performance cycle in *A Reason to Read* and in their view of how curriculum construction can be a "creative act":

> When teachers open space in the classroom for creation, they have the ability to become artists along with their students. When they design lesson plans that provide students opportunities to show they can create as a community, they invite the class to share its various ways of understanding a topic or concept. (118)

Taking on this challenge to create together as a class invites teachers and students to create an experience together that not only goes deep into the standards but deep into our memories as well.

Let's Build a Town: A Town Meeting Has Been Called

Panzenland (Peters + Franzen + Land) is a town our class creates in Food Lit as a way to completely inhabit an argument. Panzenland is debate, drama, and story all in one.

We go to Panzenland at a point in the year when the classroom community is well established—when we see that the kids value the trust we place in them, when we know there is mutual respect, and when the kids take ownership of their learning opportunities to the next level. In Panzenland we are essentially handing the classroom over to our students, so we have to be able to disagree with one another respectfully, laugh at ourselves, and take risks, and we have to believe in one another enough to know that the experience we create together will be meaningful, memorable, and, in some cases, borderline magical.

At the end of our Sweetness unit, in our third and final trimester

Taking the podium in Panzenland.

of school, the kids know that Panzenland is going to happen. We have dropped hints throughout the year about building a town and transforming our room into a town hall. Our kids have also heard about Panzenland from Food Lit alums who peek in from time to time to ask, "When is Panzenland?" This creates the greatest buzz as well as a sense of intrigue in current Food Lit students.

All we say to start our journey is "Let's build a town!" and then flash a slide of a cartoon town with the word *Panzenland* underneath. Then we hand a list of roles to each student:

Farmer—Small Scale Organic	Sanitation Worker
Farmer—Large Scale Conventional	Truck Driver
Police Officer	Social Worker
Family Doctor	Reporter
Pharmacist	Dentist
Retired _____	College Student
Forester	Artist
Nurse	Lawyer
Environmentalist	Nurse
Chef	Architect
Private Investigator	Writer
Pastry Chef	Funeral Home Owner
Stockbroker	Preacher
Temporarily Unemployed	Auto Mechanic
Kindergarten Teacher	School Lunch Worker
Candy Maker	Pastor
Musician	Real Estate Agent
Construction Worker Engineer	Police Officer
High School Principal	Business Owner
Homeless Person	Mystery
Business Owner	Mystery
Grocery Store Owner	Mystery
Bus Driver	

"Here is a list of some of the people who are going to be in Panzenland. Think about maybe your top five roles. When we draw your names out of a cup, claim your role by calling it out, and then sign the butcher paper in the front of the room. By the end of class, we would like you to sign this list as your Panzenland name. Mr. Franzen and I are going to develop a role in Panzenland, too."

The first day of Panzenland is about characterization. We flesh out the back-stories of the people in the town—the bakers, teachers, sanitation workers, park rangers, the temporarily unemployed, doctors, preachers, funeral home directors, café owners, farmers, etc.

We invite students to be quirky and creative but also to take their roles seriously. This challenge yields large discoveries and complexity. Creating personas makes us pay attention to where beliefs come from, not just for our persona but for others and ourselves as well. We see how an argument houses a spectrum of beliefs, ideas, and people—and how entering an argument is entering into this spectrum. Winning an argument doesn't always mean bringing someone over to a side; rather, winning can mean enabling someone to see an issue or the world from a new, and perhaps broader, perspective. Sometimes we even discover that we are our own opposing argument, based on a conflict between our personal and professional stances, or when we uncover moral debates such as whether to base a decision on what we believe in versus what might benefit us financially or otherwise.

We post a list of questions for students to think about as they are developing their character's backstory:

What is your name? Your age?

Are you married? Divorced? Kids? [ages and occupations]

Are you happy? Sad? Disgruntled? Grumpy? Giddy?

Where are you from originally?

What can you tell us about your childhood?

What has been a key experience in your life that maybe you don't share a lot? (Make us care.)

How did you become a/an _____ [your profession]?

How wealthy are you?

How healthy are you?

What are the most important things in your life?

What types of food do you eat? What is the backstory of sugar?

How does sweetness/sugar connect to your profession?

What are your goals? What do you want in life for you and your town?

As we circulate the room, we peek into as many of the kids' characters as possible, prodding their words, asking questions, and suggesting new dimensions for their characters so they can consider new possibilities and work through their own sets of questions and complexities. We share a few working ideas with the group so they can see the dimensions their peers are reaching. The kids are engrossed at this point. Sparks are flying. If the room could talk, it would say, "I've got this!"

Then the questions start firing:

"Can we dress up as our character when we go to Panzenland?"

"Of course you can, and you should."

"Do you have suspenders, Mr. Peters? How about a beard?"

"I do, in the prop bag in my cabinet. I'll get them for you."

"Can I bring in cupcakes? I'm a baker, and I want to bring in a sample from my business."

"I guess you'll have to."

"Can I bring in honey? I'm a beekeeper in Panzenland. My family keeps bees. Can I bring in some for the class to try?"

"Absolutely."

"I'm a candy maker; can I try to make some rock candy and bring it in?"

"You should. Let me know if I can help."

"I'm going to bring in my mixtape—I'm a rapper—and I want to let Panzenland know that I don't rap for free, Mr. Peters."

"Please bring it in."

"Can I bring in a box to put in the room for people to put in leads? I'm a private investigator."

"For sure you can. What a great idea."

Then there's a knock at the door. A messenger arrives with an announcement and a flier, which we show every student and read in dramatic fashion.

Panzenland Town Meeting Called!!
Wednesday, March 22nd, with vote on Friday, March 24th
Location: City Hall
A subsidiary of Copa-cola has offered to buy a large tract of land east of town. The 500-acre tract is a cornfield owned by old Mr. Harrow. The company proposes putting in a corn syrup refinery and soda bottling plant along with the transportation infrastructure needed for the trucking. This meeting has been called so that town members may voice their opinions on whether to approve or disapprove the land usage protocol

---

(LUP) that will determine if the plants can be built. A second meeting will reconvene the town, hear final thoughts from town members, and vote on the motion.

NOTE: Our town's decision could greatly impact the future of our small town and the next generation of Panzenlanders.
Opening Statements will be given by:
— Mr. Everett Waters, representative from DFE Beverage
— Mr. Davis Harrow, farmer and long-time Panzenland resident

The room is charged. Students begin to see the connections between the room full of reporters, bakers, teachers, waiters, police officers, homeless people, etc., and the issue at hand. There is some uneasiness and apprehension at first because all of this is new, but we bring the focus back to the roles.

"Think about how you as a baker, a teacher, a mechanic, an artist, a reporter, etc., connect to this issue. Think about how you are connected to it personally, professionally, and as a member of this community. We are going to bring the characters to life when we go to Panzenland, but first we need to explore the ways that this scenario could be good or bad for your town, for your families, and for your future. As you are completing your backstory, try to get your character close to this issue. Think about the people you connect to as well. If you are a teacher, you connect to your students, other teachers, to parents, to graduates, and the community—to sports teams, concession stands, recess and school lunch, to tax dollars and summer programs. By standing up in Panzenland, you will be standing up for others who cannot be at the meeting and all the people you connect to, so your words will carry additional weight. Bring this awareness in, and don't forget to sharpen your teeth."

The class looks at me. . . . "Sharpen your teeth? . . . What are you talking about, Mr. Peters?" So I tell them.

I tell them a story about my son, Elliot. Since it had been really cold, we were looking for games to play inside. We were pushing a play lawn mower and a small shopping cart around in the basement while holding on to spools of wrapping paper from Christmas—our swords. Elliot would stop at certain points and say, "I think I hear something." At various times he saw a sheep, a bear, or a bunny rabbit and moved on, but once he stopped and whispered, "I think I see a monster over there in the corner." I looked in the corner and started to describe the monster with him. Elliot thought that the monster could be after us. I suggested we use our swords; it seemed logical. He wasn't so sure. He thought for a minute, looked up at me, and said, "Dad, . . . maybe we should sharpen our teeth." It was a perfect idea. So we sharpened our teeth and walked toward the monster. The monster was then scared of us, and we moved on. I tell this story to remind students not to rule out possibilities and to follow their creative whims—their equivalent to sharpening their teeth.

Questions and affirmations fly, and as students see one another reaching out to pull in texts as well as props and flourishes to suggest their characters, I can see how meshing challenge, imagination, and fun creates momentum in a classroom. Not only have Joe and I given the classroom over to our kids, but our kids are moving the class forward in a way that we couldn't do on our own. Our students would be missing out on significant learning by not being able to show what they can do, and we don't want to be in their way. We won't assign any homework tonight, but the kids will take this activity home and do more unassigned work than I could ever ask them to do. They will think about Panzenland, talk about it with their friends and family, and return tomorrow with a whole slew of ideas. Students are also unleashing a part of themselves and of home that they haven't yet shown the class, even at well past the halfway point in the year. We will see this unfold in their artwork and photographs, in the accents and mannerisms they create for their characters, and in the serendipitous and in-the-moment responses that will happen only once. We encourage kids to bring their sense of humor, and to use humor as one among many rhetorical strategies. The students will show us how they are actors, artists, writers, photographers, researchers, rhetoricians, and musicians, among other things. They will prove that the most complex and ever-unfolding text is them, and we will read this in the wonderful overlap of their many talents.

When we go to Panzenland for the first time, to introduce ourselves, we go with generous ears. We aren't asking our kids to have any kind of specific role stance ready. Instead, we ask them to keep their minds open and to develop their stance as the scenario unfolds. That way we all gain the context necessary to build an informed argument. We also know from previous years that our town will have a built-in ethos, made up of the cares and concerns of all the members of the town, which includes figuring out whether the various plans of Mr. Harrow and Mr. Waters and DFE bottlers will complement or negatively affect the town. The decision we are making concerns economics, environmental impact, health and health care, quality of life, infrastructure, future generations, education, crime, and unemployment—and the town's arguments move between the short- and the long-term impacts of all these factors. We are listening for the concerns the town values most so that we can address them in our stump speeches.

On the day of our transport, we arrive with props, costumes, photos, drawings, letters, and much more. We make table tents with our Panzenland names on them so that the mayor of our town can call on us to speak. Our mayor is a surprise to the group, either a junior or a senior who has already been to Panzenland. Joe and I have given this mayor an overview of the scenario the day before, as well as an outline of the meeting and a script to read to the group. Throughout every Panzenland experience, we have many kids from previous years flag us down in the halls to ask if they can come back to Panzenland to make cameo appearances. We say yes so long as they arrive to class as their Panzen characters. This invitation helps our current students see that this strategy isn't so much our idea as it's a tradition handed down to them by previous classes, to be cared for and made better each time.

Then we ask everyone to stand up, put their left hand on their nose, and grab the tip of their right foot with their right hand.

Here's how we go to Panzenland:

1. Stand up and hold your left hand on your nose.

2. Grab the tip of your right foot with your right hand.

3. While holding on to your nose and foot, hop four times and honk each time your foot hits the ground. By the fourth honk, you should have spun in one counterclockwise circle.

4. You're in Panzenland. We generally make a big deal out of the arrival and make noises and gestures as though we're waking up from a dream.

5. To get back to Fern Creek High School (or your school), reverse everything (right hand on nose, left hand on left foot, spin and honk clockwise).

We insist that everyone who is able take part in the transport. The gesture is silly

Awkward, yes, but we're on our way to Panzenland!

The mayor of Panzenland takes the class back to Panzenland.

and awkward, but it's an effective way of giving ourselves permission to be fully in Panzenland once we get there.

When we arrive in Panzenland that first day, the complexity of the scenario immediately surfaces. We meet the schoolteacher worried about declining enrollment in her school, the park ranger who cares about the impact of air pollution on native species of plants and his declining budget, the unemployed college student who wants to be able to work in the factory so long as DFE will help her pay for her college tuition. We hear from the recently laid off factory worker, who shares the reality of factory work and worries that the same will happen in Panzenland. We welcome the rapper, who wants the factory in town to bring more people to his concerts—when he stands up, he is drinking Panzenland Punch, a DFE beverage—and he thanks DFE for using one of his songs in their commercial. We meet the cardiologist, who warns that sugar-sweetened beverages will cause arterial blockage and heart disease. We hear from the dentist, who knows that the factory will bring him more patients. He warns that there is already a soda and sweetness problem in Panzenland, with or without DFE. We meet the preacher, who quotes from 1 Corinthians 6:19–20 to reference that our bodies are temples and how we could be harming our bodies by welcoming DFE. We meet the conventional farmer, who wants to sell all his corn to DFE to refine into corn syrup, and after him speaks the small-scale organic farmer, who is worried about genetically modified corn hybridizing his organic corn—all for syrup. He says he can boil down his tomatoes instead and make Panzenland some of the best marinara sauce around—and it will be good for people.

We hear from a police officer, who knows there is a lot of crime and homelessness in Panzenland, and knows that building the factory may lead to less crime and less homelessness. The factory seems like a win, but Officer Evanswood admits to the group that he is prediabetic, and if he doesn't watch his sugars he may become insulin-dependent. Welcoming in this factory may welcome in more of the sweetness that is making him sick. He is also a husband and a father of young children. He wants his kids to be able to grow up in Panzenland, and he wants them to be able to have job opportunities so they can eventually stay in town, but he is worried that the town will change quickly, and people might move out of town if DFE pollutes the Flit River, or if the town's air quality changes. He brings to the first town meeting a message that he wants all of Panzenland to hear because this is a decision they will all have to live with for a long time. He waits for absolute silence. He gets it . . . and then he slams his hand down on the podium:

Mayor Mason with old Mr. Harrow (Jackson).

"Ladies and gentlemen, a lot of you all know me. I am a police officer, and I want you to know I'm mad. [He is soft-spoken but pounds the podium with a grand gesture and a large sound. He's worked up and the room sees this.] I'm mad because when I went to your café today [he points to a young lady in the audience who is a café owner] for lunch, they got my order wrong. I asked for a chicken sandwich and they brought me a grilled cheese. I'm mad [he pounds the podium again, this time a little more softly] because when I went to your dry cleaners [he points to the town dry cleaner] to pick up my uniforms, they were wrinkled and I clearly asked them to make sure there were no wrinkles. I'm mad because when I went to your donut shop on my late night shift [he points out the owner of the donut shop] I asked for a black coffee and got a coffee with cream and sugar instead. Panzenland! [He pounds the podium again, he has every eye, he's on a roll], you all keep getting my order wrong, and I'm mad! I keep asking you for something simple, and you cannot get things right. I have just one question for you and for this gentleman here from New York City: *[he points at the room and to me]* How can we trust him to get this factory right for our town, how can we trust him to get our order right, when we have trouble doing it ourselves?"

His flourish draws nervous laughter, silence, and then applause. To get into all the things at work in Officer Evanswood's speech is to realize just how many overlaps are happening between the rhetorical moves he's making, his awareness of and connection to his audience, and his ability to toe that thin line between inciting and exciting an audience. Cameron shows himself and all of us that he is a rhetorician who is getting the orders and the words right. His words come unexpectedly, and he makes us all believe; he uses different words and makes different moves because he is Officer Evanswood rather than Cameron, but he discovers that Cameron can make these moves, too. Officer Evanswood became real in our town while giving the rest of the class a rhetorical high five to do the same.

Pearl, an upperclasswoman and Food Lit alumna, comes back to help pass down the traditions of Panzenland.

We devote the second day in Panzenland to designing our stump speeches for the next town meeting. As well, we submit articles, news of the weird, puzzles, advertisements, want ads, crime reports, coupons, announcements, articles, etc., to our town newspaper that will be handed out to all of the Food Lit classes the next day. This gives every class a way to reach out and connect, as well as to appreciate the creativity going on from one class to another. Our town newspaper is *The Panzenland Gazette*.

The stump speeches are short, only about a minute long, and impactful. Our goal is for everyone to be able to deliver his or her speech in Panzenland. We stress a few things in particular for the speeches:

1. Start in the middle and get to the impact of your argument quickly.

2. Think beyond just creating appeals in your argument to how when these appeals overlap, as we saw yesterday, you connect to your audience in an unforgettable way. Use humor, story, hyperbole, and analogy, too, if they help you convey a point.

3. As you write, anticipate what someone who disagrees with you would say in response and be ready to offer a concession or a rebuttal in your counterargument.

4. Use strong words (diction), especially strong verbs that have a charge and an emotional impact.

5. Be the authority on what you are talking about. To do so, look things up and include statistics and research in your argument to show you have done your homework.

While we are writing, I conference with students, helping them work through their speeches. As I do, I notice that some kids are pairing up with their speeches in hand. They are either rehearsing their speeches or connecting them, because they connect in Panzenland and want to make sure their speeches are in conversation with each other. Or they're plotting secrets and surprises. . . . As I conference with kids, I see that they are preparing for curveballs in their rebuttals, and I'm trying to be mindful of these currents for my own character.

I'm plotting my moves as Everett Waters. I can see that I'm going to have a lot of people disagreeing with me based on health reasons, pollution, and the future well-being of the town, all of which the DFE factory will possibly threaten, so I need to plan to address those concerns right off the bat in my opening statements in Panzenland. As Mr. Peters, I'm encouraging students to bring in photos of graffiti they have seen in Panzenland. I'm encouraging them to do their homework on the statistics and facts they will use, and to get to know things that their character would know. I tell the dentist he should bring in that jar of teeth he's had to pull that he keeps by his door and forces himself to look at when he leaves the office. I encourage the private investigator to dig up some "dirt" on Mr. Waters's past, and I encourage the visual artist to draw a design for a mural that will depict the town before and after DFE in a not-so-flattering way.

Of course, I'm plotting against my Everett Waters self in doing this. My kids are going to be ready for me. They have written solid speeches, and I know they will present arguments with sharp teeth. I'm going to have to be ready with rebuttals and concessions, and I will go so far as to propose that DFE be sworn to a conditional (and legal) contract that requires them, under oath, to ensure that certain demands are met before they can build in Panzenland. My goal is to convince Panzenland that DFE is good for the town, and I will bring a few additional tricks, too. I'm going to secretly bring in some DFE beverages to share with the town. Maybe I'll get some Dixie cups and give everyone a taste of the future—and a test of their wills. I'll also bring along some applications with a guarantee to hire on the spot—with an immediate cash incentive for applications finished during the meeting. (I'm going to have a pocketful of play money, too.) I'll also bring in a bottle of tomato juice to see who is interested in drinking it. When I have no takers, I'll make the case for why DFE isn't in the tomato juice business—because there is little demand for it. When people demand more tomato juice, DFE will start making it. Right now, people are demanding corn syrup–sweetened sodas and they pay a lot of money to have their sodas. I'll explain to the group that this is why we make what we make . . . this, and it makes our board of directors happy.

While students are writing their speeches, I post a sign-up sheet in the room for time slots to give their stump speeches on the following day. The large butcher paper is divided into three sections. We sign up as our Panzenland names.

The top section of the sign-in sheet is for opening remarks—for Panzenlanders who have not yet decided on their stance and will listen to the arguments the next day before being convinced one way or the other. The folks who speak at the beginning are essential because they represent those who are on the fence. They set a challenge for speakers to be convincing and clear so that the town or DFE can win them over.

The middle section of the sign-in is for people who have strong stances either way. This group also has rebuttals prepared as a way to anticipate and respond to what their opposition says. During our debate, the mayor will insist that speakers be respectful and that they stay in disagreement with ideas rather than making their arguments personal. Mr. Waters and Mr. Harrow will join in this portion, chiming in to qualify their perspectives, answer questions, and respond to the concerns of the town.

The final section is for closing arguments. These are short and clever final thoughts that lead us to the moment of decision—our town's vote. At the end of the debate, we will decide our town's future. The mayor will count the votes aloud one by one while someone else tallies them. This will be tense. Usually the vote is close, very close. There are usually cheers in Panzenland, as well as disappointment.

The next day, the room is set up with two podiums facing each other, with rows of tables facing each other on each side of the podiums. We take our seats, make final edits to our speeches, gather what we need to become our persona, and make final preparations. I can tell that students are ready. I'm scared of and proud of my group at the same time. I can see that they have sharpened their teeth and are ready to dig in. We stretch, let loose of nervous energy, and then it's time. Our mayor calls us all to get up, and we magically transport, *Honk, honk, honk, honk. . . .*

"Order, order! *[a strike of the ladle to the podium]* Ladies and gentlemen of Panzenland: Today we decide how our town moves forward. I would like to thank you today for the privilege of being your mayor. And please don't forget me next November *[wink, wink]* when I go up for reelection. . . ."

And the debate begins. You will see what happens when you go to . . .

Panzenland Daily Overview

Here's a quick overview of how our Panzenland activities play out:

Day One:	Day Two:	Day Three:
Introduce the town scenario and Panzenland overview. Select roles. Begin to build your backstory/create a persona in the town. Make sure you have someone in mind for the mayor and other guest roles. Sign the town roster as your Panzenland name.	Continue to create your persona's backstory, paying close attention to all the ways you can connect your persona to the scenario. Journal entry on how your persona relates to the larger threads of this issue such as the environment, economy, quality of life, unemployment, health, crime, education, infrastructure, etc.	Make signs for your businesses to post in the room and create ads, announcements, and coupons for our town newspaper, *The Panzenland Gazette*. Discuss journal entries from previous day and link issues to your backstory. Make a list of research questions to find the answers to that will inform your argument. Set up room with one podium and tables in a half-circle around the podium.
Day Four:	**Day Five:**	**Day Six:**
Go to Panzenland for introductory statements that include how we relate to the issue. Students are focusing particularly on developing their stance, on seeing who is most convincing, and anticipating the stances and counterarguments of others.	Quick reflection of Panzenland (who made you think? And about what? and/or tip your hat to someone who stood out). Begin writing stump speeches, focusing in particular on creating appeals and the overlap of appeals.	Finish stump speeches. Submit article, puzzle, comic, column, news of the weird, town crime log, etc., to *Panzenland Gazette*. Sign up to speak in Panzenland the next day as undecided (opening), strong stances (middle), or closing thoughts (end). Set up room with two podiums for the next day.
Day Seven:	**Day Eight:**	
Go back to Panzenland to deliver stump speeches and vote on DFE. The town mayor will be guiding us through the proceedings. (You can give the mayor a script, if need be.)	Reflect on Panzenland, in particular focusing on the elements of argument that we embodied in the scenario.	

The Food Lit Flyover: A Recipe for Food Lit

The flyover works like a menu for what is happening over the course of a tri-mester. It is separate from the class syllabus. The flyover tells us what themes, questions, food pairings, and activities to expect. In short, the flyover is a way to look forward and begin mentally preparing for the trimester; it's also a way to start frontloading fun in the classroom. I try to keep the trimester's flyover brief, to let students know that things on it are subject to change.

For me, looking over past flyovers traces how the course has evolved, and how the class learns from its experiences. Based on feedback from the previous year's group, certain things stay and certain things get dropped. I try out new ideas based on student suggestions, too. I try to reach for something difficult but doable and let the class know in the process that I'm taking on challenges along-side them. The flyover makes me accountable to students—and at the beginning of the year or trimester when I have the most energy. I know that students will later remind me of things on the flyover, things that during the trimester may not seem like as good an idea considering my reservoir of energy. But I find that I need this incentive throughout the course to continue reaching. Ultimately, all the expenditure of energy is worth it because it charges and infuses the class with a collective energy. It also hands over responsibility to the class, which is important because I always realize during the trimester that I'm going to need to depend on students to help me make our experiences as wonderful as they can be; I will need to reach out to parents, too. When the class has this momentum, the collective energy is what you defer to and what makes the course turn out better than you could have imagined—or planned. You'll also discover voice within an experience, so that no two classes create quite the same experience even when they perform the same activities.

The flyover is also a way to set up what becomes a culture of invitation in the class. I am inviting and eliciting the various interests and abilities of students that they may not always have the capability to express. I'm also inviting them —and me—out of our comfort zones, to the place and the space of being will-ing to make discoveries through vulnerability, where true learning happens. In planning unit lessons and essential questions that guide those unit lessons, I'm trying to "challenge students' perspectives, inspire curiosity, and pose questions based on why things are the way they are" (78), as Jim Burke states in *What's the Big Idea?*, a book I draw on heavily as I think about planning a unit lesson. It's comfortable to sit in a chair, safe to go to the same place in class every day, but this comfort and safety seal us up and constrict growth. Instead, moving out-side of our comfort zones, or moving with complete freedom inside our comfort zones and being unafraid to show how we are talented, how we are who we are, allows for risk taking and the formation of trust, a way of showing how complex we all are and a desire to want each other to do well. The conditions for growth happen in a classroom where there is mutual support next to high challenge.

The flyover starts many conversations and lets the kids get all their insecurities out up front. As I circle the room to talk with students, I hear things like, "Do I have to act?" "I love to paint." "Mr. Peters, I do spoken word." "I write and produce my own songs; want to hear one?" "Mr. Peters, I love hot sauce—no, I *really* love hot sauce; I have some with me now." "*The Grapes of Wrath* is my mom's favorite book." "My grandma makes the best tres leches cake; I'm going to see if she will make some for class." "I love to fish." "Mr. Peters, I live on a farm and have three horses." "Can we invite our family to class?" and "My Dad has a smoker." Needless to say, teachers wouldn't often get these responses to a syllabus. When I hear these comments and conversations, I already know that students see themselves "in" the class rather than as "taking" the class. I try, at least in my heart, to frame the course as a journey we are taking, and to communicate to students that we have to be so much more than along for the ride. We have to be willing to throw ourselves into an adventure

I want to share a couple of flyovers from past trimesters so that you can appreciate the scope of how a trimester or a year of Food Lit might work. I've highlighted the seasonal by acknowledging weather and what's ripe in the garden, as well as holidays and themes that are of interest due to our location in Louisville, Kentucky. You will build your own flyovers based on your geography and landscape, your own seasonality, locality, and topics specifically related to your home.

When I create flyovers for the class, I do the following:

1. I consider closely our standards, learning targets, and the progression of reading and writing skills and skill development throughout the year from our district and school curriculum map. I look at a multitude of possibilities of texts—at how various texts are in conversation with one another across genres. I think about asking kids to bring in texts to read, especially food texts (e.g., we could read a seed packet as an informational text and a cereal box as an argument).

2. I walk outside to our garden and throughout our school's campus to think about what is in season; what can we notice, plant, harvest, process?

3. I think about the grocery store, the farmers market, our refrigerators and kitchens at home, our lunches, our school garden, etc.

4. I think about what we can pair, what we can cook, where we can have class as a result (e.g., the garden, the cafeteria, the food lab, the orchard, in Campfire, etc.), and how this will change based on the time of day.

5. I consider what we can write and create, how we can interact with each other in new ways that will encourage student voice throughout the year (as small groups, in a speed dating strategy, as partners, as individuals, as a whole class, by linking our class to another class or group, by holding an open mic, by staging a play or performance for another class).

6. I anticipate the times in the year when I can invite students to bring home to school through a dish, a small cooking demonstration, or interviews with family members (especially around holidays).

7. I think about how we can bring in people from our community and FCHS alumni to share their knowledge.

8. I wonder how we can look deeply at literature so as to see texture and contours on the page that extend into the world and into our lives and provide the opportunity to write analytically as well as informally next to the text, and, when possible, to write in the form of the text (i.e., writing our own odes, short plays, narratives, short fiction pieces, editorials, etc.). I also think about how I can invite student choice—from self-selecting independent reading books to read throughout the year to offering choice in writing prompts, etc.

9. I think about big questions and ideas, themes related to home, family, and identity.

10. I envision how we can create something as a class that will develop ownership, investment, and urgency for students, and how we can make sure that our learning is memorable (e.g., we catered a homecoming breakfast for our Alumni Association and created an experience that extended to our community and came back to the classroom in the form of a stronger community ready to take on a new challenge).

Food Lit: A Year in Flyovers

Trimester One

1. FOOD STORIES
Questions: What is good food? What is bad food? Why do we tell stories?
Food Pairing: Good food class meal

Major Readings

"The First Day" by Edward P. Jones

"Face to Face with Fugu" by Marcus Samuelsson

Food narratives written by former Food Lit students

We Found a Hat by John Klassen

"Rapunzel" by the Brothers Grimm

The Odyssey (Book 12) by Homer

"The Curious Appeal of 'Bad' Food" (from *The Atlantic)* by Irina Dumitrescu

"A Case for Eating Dog" by Jonathan Safran Foer (from *Eating Animals*)

"Oranges" by Gary Soto

"Lamb to the Slaughter" by Roald Dahl

"Dessert" by Colum McCann (Campfire)

Major Writing	**Major Actions**
Narrative writing—food narrative	Class reading of our narratives.
	Class meal—potluck.
	Create a class salad garden.

2. Seeds/Gardens

Questions: What do gardens teach us? How do stories connect us to place?
Food Pairing: Class salads from the garden and homemade dressings

Major Readings

Greek mythology: Eris's Golden Apple of Discord (illustrated story)

Chapter 1, "Desire: Sweetness / Plant: The Apple" (from *The Botany of Desire*) by Michael Pollan

Excerpts from *Banana: The Fate of the Fruit That Changed the World* by Dan Koeppel

Visual art depicting seeds and gardens

Creation story from Genesis Chapters 2 and 3

"Araby" by James Joyce

"The Garden of the Home God" Navajo story

Seed packets (with seeds that we will plant)

Garden wisdom from around the world and across time

Neruda's odes, plus a food meditation, in which we attempt to connect deeply to a food item and create an original ode based on Neruda's odes

"A Guerilla Gardener in South Central LA" TED Talk by Ron Finley

Major Writing

On-demand essay

Literature analysis essay

Major Actions

Work in school garden.

Garden Wisdom

Make homemade applesauce, mixed green salad from our garden, vinaigrette dressing, and croutons.

3. HOME
Question: How do we carry home with us?
Food Item: homemade pie

Major Readings

Excerpt about raspberry pie (from *Andy Catlett: Early Travels*) by Wendell Berry (Campfire)

"My Lucy Friend Who Smells like Corn" by Sandra Cisneros (Campfire)

"Abandoned Farmhouse" by Ted Kooser

Photos from home—analysis

Excerpts from *The Bluest Eye* by Toni Morrison (Campfire)

Excerpts from *The Kite Runner* by Khaled Hosseini

Excerpts from *The Glass Castle* by Jeannette Walls

"Those Winter Sundays" by Robert Hayden

"Appetite" by Tracy K. Smith

Informational texts on Kentucky and Louisville

Major Writing	**Major Actions**
"Where I Stand" Essay	*Home Is Here* installation

Trimester 2

1. *THE OLD MAN AND THE SEA* BY ERNEST HEMINGWAY/WATER/YELLOW RICE WITH PLANTAINS

Questions: What journeys are we on? Where does strength come from when people count us out?

We will take a critical look at Hemingway's text. In particular, we will pay close attention to Santiago's vision and journey, and we will analyze relationships between humans and water in the book and at local, national, and global levels. We will also be creating a visual representation of the text as a class by painting a watercolor of a scene in the novel, then pairing that scene with a quote from the text and creating a gallery of these paintings that will help us to see the text in color. In addition, we will make and share in the meal that Manolin brings to Santiago before he goes out fishing. We will write our own original poems inspired by the texts we read, and bring in an artifact from our lives that connects to one of the themes running throughout the story.

Additional Works

Articles from major newspapers related to a water issue (informational texts)

The Old Man and the Sea (animated video) directed by Aleksadr Petrov

Water wisdom quotes and response

"The Distance of the Moon" by Italo Calvino (short story)

Excerpts from *Four Fish* by Paul Greenberg

Poems—"The Fish" by Elizabeth Bishop, "The Salmon Fisher to the Salmon" by Seamus Heaney, "Ode to a Large Tuna in the Market" by Pablo Neruda, "The Fish" by Mary Oliver, "Miracle Fair" by Wislawa Szymborska, and other selected poems

Major Writings

Literary analysis essay based on *OMS*—Synthesis paper: Connect *OMS* to one other text of your choice

Original poems

Major Actions

Class cooking

Create a class gallery for our watercolor paintings

2. CURIOSITY + CHALLENGE PROJECT

We will compile a list of all of the things we are curious about, and we will magically turn this into a great big (doable) challenge! We will give ourselves permission to learn about and/or do something we have always wanted to do. We will make ourselves accountable to each other by checking in on each other, and we will dust off any fear that is keeping us from facing what we know we love. We will take a risk, be daring, and we will learn a lot. (This project will be conducted over the holiday break!) Mr. Peters is creating one too!

Major Texts

"A Curious Boy" TED Talk by James Cameron + scores of samples of and artifacts from previous Curiosity + Challenge Projects

Major Writing

Curiosity + Challenge reflection and brief presentation to the class after holiday break

3. *THE PIANO LESSON* BY AUGUST WILSON/MIGRATION/RECIPES FROM THE GREAT MIGRATION

We will explore "culture" and the movement of culture. We will especially be focused on the Great Migration and cultural productions about and from the Great Migration, including painting, music, poetry, drama, and food. We will look at what travels with culture and see how a family like the Charles family in *The Piano Lesson* represents not only the movement of culture but also the deep connection to home, identity, history, story, place, and family. We will trace movements of culture through these works and extend our reading of *The Piano Lesson* to look for ways in which traditions and themes from the Great Migration extend out to present-day artistic representations.

Additional Works

"Everyday Use" by Alice Walker (short story)

Excerpts from *The Warmth of Other Suns* by Isabel Wilkerson

Excerpts from *A Raisin in the Sun* by Lorraine Hansberry (Campfire)

Paintings from Jacob Lawrence's Migration Series and by Aaron Douglas and Romare Bearden

Poems—"The Great Migration" by Yusef Komunyakaa, "Say Grace" by Rita Dove

Recipes from the National Museum of American History's series Cooking Up History (section titles "Food and the Great Migration" and "The Food of Jazz")

Music and lyrics from blues, jazz, and rap artists

Raisin toast and *A Raisin in the Sun*: A food pairing for Campfire.

Major Writings

Original poetry inspired by paintings by Jacob Lawrence, Aaron Douglas, and Romare Bearden

Literary analysis paper

Major Actions

Create an original work of art (e.g., a collage, a painting, a poem, a dish, a song, etc.) to put in conversation with *The Piano Lesson*.

Original performances based on and inspired by the play.

Class Tea: Our trimester will conclude with our very own Valentine's Day class tea. We will decorate our classroom and transform it into a café. We will sign up to bring homemade items to the tea, and we will write sonnets, haiku, and limericks related to love and heartbreak and display them on the walls, on the tables as place settings, and in our class poetry anthology as well. Finally, we will reflect on the tea and on the trimester in a letter to Mr. Peters.

Major Readings

Shakespearean sonnets, haiku, limericks, and other poetry to serve as models for our own writing.

Beginning of Trimester 3

1. ARGUMENT

We will start our investigation of argument with a review of the rhetorical situation and rhetorical appeals. Our reading will focus on annotating, as well as weighing in on arguments in all types of forms—speeches, editorials, poems, objects, and many others—in order to test Andrea Lunsford's claim that "everything's an argument."

Major Readings

TED Talks

New York Times student editorials

Historical speeches

Major Writings

Rhetorical analysis paper

Editorial in the style of *New York Times* student editorial competition with the goal of entering this year's competition

Major Actions

Class debate

2. *SALT SUGAR FAT* BY MICHAEL MOSS/SWEETNESS/PANZENLAND

We will read and analyze Moss's essay "I Want to See a Lot of Body Bags" and look at how he constructs an argument, as well as how he examines the rhetoric of sweetness by examining a sweet food item. We will look at our relationship with salt, sugar, and fat and the ways that we are the audience for advertising. We will jump on the sweetness carousel to determine our sweetness preference via taste test, conduct sugar conversions of our favorite snacks, look at how the process of sugar works, consider sugar and the body, and look closely at the rhetoric of breakfast cereal and candy. As well, we will decode what makes a lot of the foods that we crave so appealing by conducting a snack food analysis. This thematic unit will conclude with a visit to Panzenland, where we will create a town and debate an issue related to sweetness.

Additional Works

"Hansel and Gretel" by the Brothers Grimm

Rhetorical analysis of cola ads

Excerpts from *The Road* by Cormac McCarthy

Excerpts from *The Dorito Effect* by Mark Schatzker

Excerpts from *The Grapes of Wrath* by John Steinbeck (Campfire)

"Linoleum Roses" (from *The House on Mango Street*) by Sandra Cisneros

"Teach Every Child about Food" TED Talk by Jamie Oliver

Major Writings

Panzenland stump speeches

Panzenland reflection

Major Action

Create our own class town

I have taught *Fences* by August Wilson, *A Raisin in the Sun* by Lorraine Hansberry, *Fahrenheit 451* by Ray Bradbury, *Othello* or *A Midsummer Night's Dream* by William Shakespeare, and *The Great Gatsby* by F. Scott Fitzgerald either in place of one of the other larger works in this flyover or as the larger work that wraps up the year after Panzenland. Throughout the school year, my students and I read in self-selected independent reading books from a class list of pre-AP and AP texts. At the end of the year, students write a final paper and create an engaging presentation about one of the independent reading books they have completed. This gives us all a chance to share in our reading journey for the year and compile a list of possible books for summer reading. We finish our year with a celebration—either in the form of a class breakfast, a picnic, or a class cookout and field day—along with a Food Lit end-of-year slide show and a final reflection.

The flyovers are a guide to help you see what a Food Lit year can look like, as well as the sequence of activities in the class. The flyovers change from year to year, and even during the year, but the strategies described in this chapter remain a constant. These strategies help the class become a community and enable us to read far beyond the surface of texts, to listen to one another to understand, to respect each other even when we disagree, and to become better at asking our questions and articulating our thoughts in discussion, on the page, and beyond.

By creating an environment in which high challenge, high support, and care live next to each other, we set up the conditions to value and celebrate growth—as readers, writers, thinkers, teachers, speakers, and our own unique selves. On days when not everything goes according to plan, or when there is some difficulty or struggle in the class, the resilience of the community helps us move through and move beyond the problem—and to grow stronger as a result. As I reflect on each year of the class, I am convinced that we are only scratching the surface of what is possible. I am propelled to move the class forward into the possibility of what Food Lit can become and is becoming, as envisioned by students in their ideas for the class and as confirmed by the memories we all share of the joy, positivity, and enthusiasm that I want to carry in to the next year, in an even more compelling way. I am honored to share this work in progress with you, and for you to carry this into your own classrooms.

Some Additional (Essential) Food Lit Reading

Here are some titles that have been indispensable for me, either as inspiration, as sources of food writings, as cooking resources, or as works that expanded and changed the way I think about food. I read and re-read them.

For a treasure trove of poetry related to food, I recommend *The Hungry Ear: Poems of Food and Drink* edited by Kevin Young.

For learning to cook from scratch in a very friendly way, I recommend any cookbook written by Molly Katzen, especially the cookbook that started my whole cooking adventure when I received it as a college graduation present (and later inspired a pilgrimage to the Moosewood restaurant), the classic *Moosewood Cookbook*.

For about three cookbooks that (are personal favorites and) are solid as examples of narrative and instructional writing, as well as sources of some of the most delicious recipes out there, I recommend *The Art of Simple Food* by Alice Waters, *Jerusalem* by Yotam Ottolenghi and Sami Tamimi, and *The Zuni Cafe Cookbook* by Judy Rodgers.

I also recommend the following books that have broadened my view of the food landscape: *Bringing It to the Table: On Farming and Food* by Wendell Berry, *The Omnivore's Dilemma: A Natural History of Four Meals* by Michael Pollan, *The Third Plate: Field Notes on the Future of Food* by Dan Barber, *The Language of Food: A Linguist Reads the Menu* by Dan Jurafsky, *Tacopedia: The Taco Encyclopedia* by Déborah Holtz and Juan Carlos Mena, and the classic *What to Eat* by Marion Nestle.

Saying Yes beyond the English Classroom and beyond the School Day

Stepping Out

Naturally, the Food Lit course has a lot to do with bringing food into the classroom. If you are reading this book for ways to do that, this chapter will show you new ways to incorporate food and how to move outside the classroom and into other disciplines. But by now you have realized that Food Lit is also about how to create a community of learners, read the texts of our lives and surrounding world, empower student voice and actions, and design a classroom that unlocks passions, including your own. This chapter expands on these benefits by exploring the other courses, clubs, and infrastructure of the Food Studies program that continue to empower students through a multidisciplinary approach that can be applied in any classroom.

Going into our tenure at Fern Creek High School, Brent and I didn't have a grand vision or a theoretical framework. We had some understanding of what people had done in the past and were currently doing that engaged kids. We knew what we cared about and had an idea about what we wanted to see in the classroom. We did not forsee how the idea would grow and how students would run with it. Where they took the course often led us to asking for strange permissions, such as *Can we throw spears at a hay-bale bison while standing around a fire on a January day? Can we travel to the Navajo Nation to explore foodways? Can we tap maple trees around campus for syrup? What happens if we can make a better school lunch? How can I start a garden at home? Can I have yeast to make this at home? What do I say when I meet Prince Charles?* It also led us to develop skills and fulfill roles we didn't know we needed as teachers: fundraisers, travel agents, public speakers, social networkers, social workers, construction managers, caterers—you get the idea. However, learning on the job and from your students makes teaching matter. We realized through our learning and their engaged work that it matters to them, too.

The strategies in this book are not new. We started off observing the basic

Maslow hierarchy of needs. If you are hungry, have a strawberry from the garden or treat from Cooking Club. If you feel sad or insecure, have a handshake and let's talk about it for a minute. Through validating lived texts and inviting students' homes into the classroom, we embrace culturally responsive teaching while fostering critical thinking and building student empowerment within their community. Although called Food Studies, the program is a weird mash-up of the current push for nutrition, garden, place-based, and sociological culinary studies that have been found to tie students to the ground beneath them, to their bodies, and to the subsequent interaction between those two. Similar programs include Alice Waters's Edible Schoolyard program, many grandma's kitchens, farm-to-school programs nationwide supported by Slow Food and Cooperative Extension offices, and increasingly at schools that are trying to solve the need for local food in their cafeterias while providing meaningful volunteer opportunities for students.

The bottom line is that we didn't approach our work at Fern Creek as academics. We approached it more like the young kid cooking spaghetti and slinging noodles at the wall to see if it sticks: full of curiosity, doubt, and a sense that you will be told to stop at any minute (BTW, if it sticks, it's done, and be ready to clean up a mess when you teach that lesson). This book is a collection of our dried wall noodles and the sheepish encouragement to throw food at the wall no matter whether it's fusilli, gnocchi, or couscous. I guarantee that you will find others who are willing to experiment with you and be ready to celebrate when a strategy, lesson, or perspective sticks in your classroom community.

This chapter first takes you through strategies that work to create community in a classroom. Some start with food as the central experience; others build the relationships between students and with the teacher so that you can cook, garden, and have collective ownership in a classroom. Then, like the flyovers for Food Lit, overviews of Global Issues I, II, and Advanced and Food Sociology courses demonstrate how food can "look" as a unit, as an authentic project-based learning experience, as a class outside of the English classroom (you will see how food can make a disciplinary bridge), and as the structural and ideological foundation that allowed us to build and maintain a garden, plant an orchard, build benches and a pavilion, cook for one another and the community, and perform other actions that made people ask, "How the heck did that happen?" We explore some of the multidisciplinary projects from these courses. With student voices showcasing the individual's experience throughout the program, the last part of this chapter explores the aspects of the program that took place outside of the school day and classroom, focusing on the the Environmental and Cooking Clubs. Although the Food Studies program as a whole is diverse, overlapping, noisy, and seemingly disjointed from a traditional educational perspective, what you will find in every voice heard here is teachers and students saying yes to learning as multidisciplinary, enjoyable, and meaningful.

Empowering Students Starts with a Handshake

The Food Lit class and extended community would not have existed or sustained itself without the intentional construction of social capital and inherent trust that comes from seeing each other as having value, having compassion, and having the best interests of each person at its core. For some students, the most important lessons they took away from Food Lit had nothing to do with English or food. For some it was how to navigate the complex dynamics of high school relationships and the ability to make decisions for themselves. For some it was how to code-switch, to be able to talk to adults at school in a way that seemed polite while going home to a completely different set of expectations. For some it was knowing that there are people who care about them and will listen. For some it was the importance of being able to look someone in the eye, confidently grip their hand, and say good morning.

When the bell rings for the first class of every subject of every trimester that Brent and I teach, we tell all of the students to leave the room. At first the students look bewildered. The first day of class is supposed to be quiet, passive, a monotone reading of a syllabus, a litany of expectations that have to be tested and tried in the coming weeks to see what the teacher is made of. Brent and I just walk out of the room. The students follow, and we ask them to line up in front of the lockers, shoulder to shoulder. At this point, I tell my story of how I know that handshakes and standing at the door as a greeter matter. As you read, think about how you welcome students to your class and how their stories enter your classroom.

"Welcome to _____ [Food Lit, Global Issues, Food Sociology]. You are about to become part of a community that has been founded in care, sustained through hard work, and maintained by people who expect you to respect what you have inherited. The classroom is a sacred space that is not defined by four walls or two bells, but by the people, voices, and minds that are in it." Brent and I then introduce ourselves by name.

"Upon entering this classroom, you also are entering into this sacred place and journey, and as you would approach a temple, shrine, church, mosque, or anything of importance, there are rituals that must be maintained. In this space, we greet each other.

"There are three main reasons why this ritual is in place. First, this space, this class, is different from most, as you will see, and it must be defined by what it is not. It is not the hallway, and it requires a different set of behaviors. It is not a sit-and-get class, and you must prepare yourselves to think, talk, and be critical. It is not home, where you are either a parent or a child, but a place where we are all learners. The greeting helps you define where you are. Second, many students go through the entire day without having meaningful contact with another human being. You may bump into someone in the hall or get called on in class, but these interactions rarely touch the humanity and true self that is within each of you. I have seen students come into the building, day in, day out, who do not have meaningful human interactions. In a reality like that, a student doesn't learn anything meaningful or grow as a person. Third, and probably most important, as we start to see each other as human beings who have value, we must understand that we all bring home, mom and dad, brother and sister, the fight from last week, birthdays, grandpa in the hospital, empty cupboards, a new sibling, insecurities, getting yelled at last class, and the pressures of the future with us, in our heads and on our minds, and that sometimes, these seem a little more important than the rules delineating the use of semicolons.

"Let me tell you a story that offered me insight into this third reason for our daily greeting. I taught seventh grade for four years, and during that time I started standing at the door to the outside to greet students as they got off the bus. One Monday morning, Kenneth, a student I had in class, got off the bus, walked toward me, and as I put out my hand, he looked me straight in the eyes and calmly said, 'Fuck you.' (I use "FU" with students.) With a certain degree of disbelief, since Kenneth and I had a really solid relationship and also it was Monday morning and I was still waiting for the coffee to fully kick in, I asked Kenneth to try this again, and again I put out my hand. He said, "Fuck you, Franzen!," and I saw that his calm face was slowly breaking into one of pain, desperation, and tears. I asked him to walk down the hall with me, away from other students, who were starting to stare. At the end of the hall, I stopped and, while looking him in the eyes, said, 'It's Monday morning. I haven't seen you for the past two days. We left school last Friday with our relationship intact. I know you aren't angry at me, and it's not me those words are meant for. What is going on?' Through tears, Kenneth told me about his drunk dad coming home and hitting his mom and his brother. Kenneth hid upstairs from Sunday morning until Monday morning, until he could sneak out to school. He was hungry, scared, tired. To him, school was a place where he could be safe. To him, I was an adult male to whom he could say what he needed to say and not get hit. We made sure Kenneth got help.

"However, I reflected a lot on that day and thought about what could have happened if I hadn't been at the door that Monday morning. Kenneth still would have come to school full of those emotions, pain and rage. He would have gone to his first period class and sat there with a calm face hiding the explosive weekend inside. A student would have made a joke, bumped into him—any minor slight would do it—and Kenneth would have erupted. The teacher would have been shocked and appalled, and marched Kenneth to the principal, angry that the class had been disrupted, that phone calls would have to be made, that the other teachers would talk about the fight in her room, that paperwork would need to be filled out and the lesson would have to be redone. Kenneth would be putting up walls to protect himself and would feel ashamed that he had acted out, know that people would look at him differently, that the administration would see him as a "bad kid" even though he tried so hard, and that he would be suspended. Sent home. To a father who now had a reason to focus on him, and Kenneth would have nowhere to go. I am so glad that I was told to f* myself that morning. Greeting Kenneth might be one of the best things I have ever done as a teacher."

At this point, the students lined up against the lockers are silent. They have a stranger in front of them who isn't supposed to smile, let alone get emotional and vulnerable on the first day of school by saying that the best thing he's ever done as a teacher is accept a phrase that we aren't allowed to say in school. Confusion at the beginning of a new course is a great way to start building something new, special, and important when people are accustomed to the same old show.

"I know that many of you face challenges like Kenneth did. I hope that you don't experience anything as severe, but in my experience as a teacher, these things happen. Know that when we greet each other, look each other in the eye and ask each other how we are doing, we mean it. You cannot be the student you can be if you have the baggage of life weighing you down and demanding your attention."

With this, we introduce instructions on the three types of greeting: (1) a handshake—firm grip, eye contact, right hand, no broken knuckles; (2) a fist bump—blow it up, creative interpretations are encouraged, snail; and (3) a high five—don't demean me because I'm short, windmill Zack Morris high five gets five extra life points. We greet each other with our names in a rotating circle and reenter the classroom on this first day as a community with a shared experience, a shared set of expectations, a value placed on storytelling, and a baseline for the compassion that we will have for one another.

Pancake Breakfast

The first week of any class is pretty quiet. Students are trying to feel the teacher out and figuring out who will fill which roles. The quiet tension can lull teachers into the misperception that the rest of the semester will be equally calm and quiet. What I have found is that this is the perfect time to break those traditional tropes of the first week. So, after kicking all the kids out of the room the first day and shaking hands, we make pancakes within the first week.

Now, this isn't your traditional cooking demonstration. I put a stack of recipes (I have used many different recipes, but my advice is to go simple) in the center of the room next to all of the ingredients. I have placed bowls at workstations around the room next to slips of paper that list their three-person teams. When everyone is at their station, I give the rules: (1) if you create an unsafe situation, you will not cook the rest of the semester; (2) all group batches of batter will be put together as a class batter at the end; and (3) only Otis Redding will be heard over my speakers. I then let them loose.

Some students are lost. Some are petrified with the knowledge that if they mess up they will ruin pancakes for everyone else. Some pull on experiences from home. What has never failed to happen is that the students become teachers for one another. They fill in each other's gaps in knowledge. I see grandpa and mom and dad and aunt come out in my kids from their years of looking over counters in the kitchen. I see students realizing that making pancakes isn't some magical skill, but something they can do with minimal time, effort, and ingredi-

Kyree, Dane, and Shamar make the class batter.

Dennis on the griddle.

ents. For the groups that have issues, I offer some hints and guidance. If a situation gets really bad, I will toss the bowl, Gordon Ramsey style, and have them start over. The groups that are killing it I let loose to make multiple batches to meet the law of averages for pancake batter quality.

The students think they have made pancake batter. What we actually did was break the conventional dynamics of a classroom. I put them in charge. I offered risk with an authentic reward. I made them teachers for one another. They then defined what the class would be. For the rest of the course, I will be only a guide.

The next day I have three electric griddles set up, and the first six students to arrive become pancake flipper teams. I've posted a list on the board of what we need to have the class meal: tables arranged in a long row, chairs pushed in around tables, syrup out, strawberries cut, plates put out, silverware set, chairs counted, and then everyone seated. There is some downtime: get students talking, challenge the pancake flippers, make outrageous claims about griddle spacing efficiency, awkwardly introduce students to each other—before you know it, the batter has been made into cakes and the students are waiting to eat. Although the flippers have snuck a cake or two, be clear about the rule that no one eats until everyone is seated and thanks are given.

I'm sure some readers gasped when they read "thanks," with its religious overtones, but it's the teacher's job to explain what it means to be thankful, how to appreciate one another, and how to be comfortable saying so no matter our language, religion, color, or culture. We go around the table, no exceptions but come-back-tos allowed. You would be amazed at what we learn about one another in the first week when we're sitting around a table with strangers we've

Camdan, Pearl, Don, and Iishe flipping cakes.

just cooked with and our mouths are anticipating pancakes. We get to know those strangers, and the feast begins.

This early activity has become a staple of all my classes. It challenges the norms while also becoming a shared text that can be referenced throughout the semester as we talk about nutrition, compassion, community, love, work, and responsibility, and as we want to yell at the person across the circle from us. For my students, it immediately shows them what their class can look like and how the expected roles in the room can be shifted so quickly to make a community of collaborators, storytellers, and thinkers.

The Circle

Most students take some time to adjust to not having a desk. On most days, my classroom has the large tables pushed to the edges of the room, with a large circle of thirty-two to thirty-six chairs of various shapes and sizes, along with a projector, computer, set of props, and a performance area, in the center. There are no desks to hide behind. No tables to lay a head down on. Nothing to hide hands busy on a phone. Students are looking directly across the room at another person.

I spend most of my time in the circle facilitating conversation, presenting information, and, if they are writing on clipboards or notebooks, running from student to student to kneel in front of them to work through a concept. As a teacher, this setup can be challenging. You can't sit down all class period; you need to be constantly up and moving. You always have your back to some students, which demands student ownership of the class, behavior, and work. It can be tiring and intense and make you feel as though you are surrounded. It's also an arrangement that a class can easily shift to, or become one more tool for the classroom to use in facilitating discussions or functioning as a community.

Although this classroom formation has its complications, the payoffs are huge. I see increased student engagement. Whether because they don't have a table to fall asleep on or because they feel exposed without laminate wood to hide behind, students are awake more, pay more attention, and tend to share, challenge, and talk more. For classroom management purposes, this arrangement means I can immediately ask students why they've pulled out their phones. Sixty percent of the time, phone use leads to an exciting extension of the topic they have been researching; 30 percent requires a quick reminder to pay attention and fight the pull of social media; the last 10 percent usually reveals a serious issue that a student needs help with and to talk about. Bottom line, the exposure of the circle allows me to be a more effective and efficient educator, classroom manager, and social worker.

However, the most important part of this classroom organization is the conversation it encourages. Any teacher who has done a Socratic seminar knows the power of conversation, as well as the challenge of getting students comfortable talking to one another and the danger of a conversation getting away from the guidance of the teacher. Holding class most days in this circle of chairs allows students to see this arrangement as normal and to believe that the expectation of conversation is something they are capable of. And after these norms are set, a positive classroom community has been built, and respectful, deep conversations that address meaningful issues that matter in society and to the students become a daily occurrence.

As the trimester continues, consistent student engagement in the circle builds a capacity for conversations that loop back to past student ideas, opinions, and shared texts. Because students have become a community in the circle, their internalized lived texts, which often are hidden away in other school settings, emerge to enrich the learning experience for everybody. An example of this was a simple current event update on a Monday about a chemical attack on Syrian civilians and a US missile attack in retaliation. I provided background information and set the stage, and then asked what the kids thought. The usual hands went up quickly, asking the basic information and clarification questions while also setting the basic moral and values-based perspectives. Next came the larger questions, those looking for the difference between killing someone with chemicals versus a piece of metal, the difference between murder and killing someone with the government behind you, the larger geopolitical narrative that surrounds a missile attack, the biological impact and process of a chemical attack, what gives a nation or individual the right to take another person's life. In forming these questions, students brought up how our perspectives might be shaped by our cultural lenses, that we must break the chains that tie us to the floor of Plato's allegorical cave to get an unfettered view of universal concepts such as war and death. I often had to hide my excitement as students started to step back and look more objectively at what is taken as a norm in American society, and I offered David Foster Wallace's fish analogy from *This Is Water* to do so. For those not familiar with Wallace's analogy, it goes like this: Two young fish are swimming by an older fish, who asks, "How's the water?" The two young fish look at each other and ask, "What is water?" This analogy gave students the impetus to wonder what their "water" is, pushing against what is assumed, acculturated, and passively adopted.

These conversations are interdisciplinary, emotional, soul-searching, formative, and constant. Often we are interrupted by the bell, and my lesson for the day gets pushed until tomorrow (luckily, this is an elective where I can do so). Three out of five days a week there is an after-class circle, with students stepping into the center of the circle to continue to process and hash out their own thoughts. Sometimes this time after class is when I need to help students diffuse differences in perspective, which is when I model how I was taught adults are supposed to process conflict—by being respectful, by listening, by being open-minded, and by shaking hands while acknowledging the other person is a human being with a brain, emotions, and people they love. Inevitably there are students who will disagree with each other. Developing the skills to talk to and not past each other is more important now than ever. The skills built into and as a result of the class circle are what allow a person to resolve conflict and improve the world around them.

The biggest win from implementing the circle is showing students that learning and a classroom can look different. Learning doesn't have to consist of worksheets, rows, and textbooks. It isn't a one-way transaction in which information goes in and comes out in the form of a graphite-filled circle at the end of the year. Students see learning and knowledge move around the room and throughout time as ideas from a month ago resurface, or when they realize that a mathematical concept or a trivial fact they learned in science or social studies actually has meaning in an authentic context and explored with the voices and minds of thirty-plus peers.

Once the norms of the circle are set and students are comfortable in the setting, the circle can move anywhere. It can take place outdoors on benches or in the greenhouse. Every project ends in a circle so that we can reflect, critique, and celebrate. The circle becomes part of the class culture, and the expectations of dialogue and interaction go with the students to their next class, to the cafeteria, and to home. More important, it takes our class to new places of connective analysis where students are comfortable sharing their vulnerabilities and finding support, the stereotypes and assumptions of others are laid bare by others' life experiences, and young people learn how to question one anothers' ideas and opinions to make them stronger. To start, teach them to ask the question "Why?"

Cultural Lens

One of the first activities (after making pancakes, of course) that we do in Global Issues and Food Sociology is the cultural lens. This activity allows us to acknowledge and recognize that each of us views the world around us differently and that we all could potentially live in different realities. This process also helps students see food, identity, culture, and the individual as all tied together and worthy of in-depth study. The concept of a cultural lens comes from the fields of anthropology and sociology, where it's used to identify the larger cultural influences on how the world is seen and interacted with. For my courses, I use the cultural lens concept to help students begin to see the larger cultural and societal influences that might shape their realities, opinions, situations, and perspectives. In this capacity, the cultural lens gets a little more individualistic and delves into a degree of amateur pyschology.

We draw and individually explore the diagram in Figure 3.1. In the lens, we put gender, religion, age, race, family, life experiences, jobs, roles, location, language, sexual orientation, and whatever else is deemed to be a large determining piece of one's identity. I go down the list and give rationales for how each element could change how a person views the world or how the world might treat you differently. I outline different expectations of boys and of girls in US society. I talk about different rules and values of different religions. We talk about how a senior citizen might see the world differently than a child. Race is always a challenging topic in that many believe we are a postracial society even while we live in a world of invisible—and sometimes visible—racial tension and conflict. Challenging someone's understanding is never easy. I try to do it and am often saved by students of color sharing some personal stories of how skin

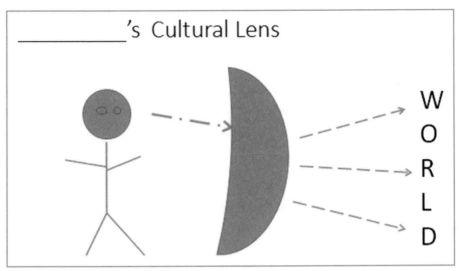

FIGURE 3.1. Basic diagram to help explain and explore a cultural lens.

color has shaped their relationship with society. These become conversations that last the entire year. I give examples of the elements that constitute the cultural lens, but students start to get the idea by the time I model it: male, raised Christian, age thirty-three, white, dysfunctional Brady bunch family and in the middle, father committed suicide, construction worker then teacher, Pennsylvania to Virginia to Kentucky, English and bit of Spanish, straight, and loves food, the outdoors, and my wife.

The students dive in. They ask clarifying questions, expecting answers. I say I can't give them answers because *they* are the texts. They are the only person who can tell them how they view the world. This process naturally leads to students questioning how these characteristics might have shaped them and their opinions. It leads students to compare their lens with their neighbors' and to ask questions. We often end up in some really interesting and revealing conversations.

As students finish these up, I ask whether two people could be in the same social situation, see it differently, and both be right. We start to try on perspectives and realize that one person may not be able to define a true reality. The conclusion we reach as a class is that each person's perspective is unique, valid, and important. The class also always gains the understanding that when we have class conversations and argue, we are talking to educate the other and not to prove who is right or wrong. With that understanding, the conversations become a collaboration instead of combat or competition. Our cultural lenses come up in every class conversation, whether in relation to the Allegory of the

Cave or trying to understand David Foster Wallace, in Current Event Fridays and in long-term projects; they become a new norm in how we talk about the world. The understandings earned through the cultural lens also empower students to take on the tasks for which their lives are the texts, as in the Food Heritage project. Without this activity of basic self and and social awareness, it is incredibly difficult to take on the meaningful work discussed throughout this book.

Questions to Chew On

1. How are you creating an inclusive community of learners on the first day, in the first week, and for the first unit?

2. How are you helping students develop a critical lens and agency in navigating their world?

3. If you could make a special handshake, what would it look like? (One involved hooking ankles and hopping in a circle this year.)

4. How are you using classroom community to take learning to new levels?

Flyovers

Each of the courses in the Food Studies program builds skills and uses strategies that reinforce community, develop student capital, and continue to push for more opportunity for student empowerment, voice, and action. In the following sections, you'll find the big picture structure of the other Food Studies classes. Some are explicitly food-centric and others incorporate food throughout in community-building activities, days in the garden, service learning, philosophical conversation, or unit themes. The pinnacle of these courses is Global Issues Advanced, where many students who have taken Food Lit, Global Issues I and II, and/or Food Sociology demonstrate the skills and culture of the program. The underlined projects and strategies are showcased later in the chapter.

Global Issues I, II, and Advanced

Structure of Curriculum for a 12-Week Trimester Global Issues I Course

Unit 1: Introduction—2 weeks

- Students will explain how cultural differences can influence national actions, explore and question current cultural perspectives within American society, and identify their own cultural biases and perspectives.

• Assessment: Self-Analysis Essay

Unit 2: Where Do I Want to Be?—1 week

• Students will identify a lifelong goal, develop a detailed action plan to reach that goal, and evaluate the current education system in reaching their goals.

Unit 3: Exploring Altruism—2 weeks

• Students will describe the controversy behind the concept of altruism and evaluate the role of altruism in their own lives and community.

• Assessment: Altruism Essay

Unit 4: Social and Economic Justice—2 weeks

• Students will develop working definitions of social and economic justice and use those definitions to explore and analyze local, national, and global realities.

Unit 5: Food Justice—2 weeks

• Students will develop working definitions of food justice; use those definitions to explore and analyze local, national, and global food realities; and design and implement a food drive.

Unit 6: Environmental Justice—2 weeks

• Students will develop working definition of environmental justice; use those definitions to explore and analyze local, national, and global realities; and design and implement a recycling drive.

Structure of Curriculum for a 12-Week Trimester Global Issues II Course

Unit 1: Introduction—3 weeks

• Students will study and analyze Plato's Allegory of the Cave, tenets of existentialism, and David Foster Wallace's *This Is Water*.

• Set up routines: TED Talk of the Week, stat of the week, current events, outside

• Assessment: Essay

Unit 2: Major Global Issues—3 weeks

- Students will participate in a crash course on issues: climate change (small behavior change or system management), violence, hunger, income inequality, education, school-to-prison pipeline, knowledge of cooking, racism.

- Introduce the long-term project (LTP)

- Assessment: Choose issue, research, action plan, lesson

Unit 3: Outdoor Classroom—3 weeks

- Students will explore and debate the theory of nature deficit disorder, design an outdoor education project, and execute it.

- Outdoor project: Rebuild wetlands, label trees, garden, student directed

- Assessment: Physical project and daily log

- Field trip: Camp Crooked Creek adventure camp

Unit 4: Food and Community/Project Work—3 weeks

- Students will explore the connections between food, poverty, culture, justice, and inequality through reading community-based texts ("Fat City" [Laidman], excerpts of Louisville's Health Equity Report (Arno and Rock), Dare to Care [food bank]) and engage in conversation focusing on the concept of fat-shaming versus health.

- Assessment: Reflection and service documentation, present projects

Structure of Curriculum for a 12-Week Trimester Global Issues Advanced Course

Week 1: Introduction

- Students will complete a Global Issues review assessment, collaborate on a philosophy crash course, develop a baseline set of knowledge of current events, and explore the key themes for the course.

Weeks 2–11: Working as a Community

- Students will contribute to a preset or individual long-term project, own and maintain a FCHS garden bed and care for the chickens, collaborate to build and maintain a learning forest on campus, research and dissect theme-based weekly current events, and contribute weekly to a class blog.

- <u>Sample Week Design:</u>

  Monday: introduce topics, explore definitions and preconceptions

  Tuesday: class project work day

  Wednesday: LTP work day

  Thursday: LTP, current event work day

  Friday: current event and snack

Week 12: Presentations of LTP

Food Sociology

Structure of Curriculum for a 12-Week Trimester Course

Unit 1: Basics of American Society, Kitchen Rules, and Food—weeks 1 and 2

- Students will be able to identify tools in the kitchen, define/discuss the key terms of sociology in regard to American society, and identify/discuss the major food issues of modern America.

Unit 2: Human Nature and Hunter-Gatherer Societies-—week 3

- Students will be able to discuss the concept of human nature in reference to hunter-gatherer societies, explore the Paleolithic diet, and hunt and eat as a hunter-gatherer through participating in the <u>hunter-gatherer games</u> and making bison stew.

Unit 3: Social Structure and the Neolithic Revolution—week 4

- Students will be able to discuss the concepts of social structure, status, and specialization in regard to the Neolithic Revolution.
- Students will be able to build a Neolithic civilization through a student-generated simulation and analyze the process and <u>bake a loaf of bread</u>.

Unit 4: Genocide and the Columbian Exchange—week 5

- Students will be able to discuss the concept of genocide in regard to the Columbian exchange and <u>make/use a pizza to teach the Columbian exchange</u>.

MIDTERM: <u>The Food Heritage Project</u>

- Students will be able to analyze a piece of my own food heritage as a sociologist and make a dish from my family's heritage.

Unit 5: Slavery and the American South—weeks 6 and 7

- Students will be able to explore the institution of slavery and its legacy, and research, contextualize, and make southern cuisine and "soul" food.

Unit 6: Capitalism, Communism, and the Industrial Revolution—week 8

- Students will be able to debate the pros and cons of communism and capitalism in regard to the Industrial Revolution and modern America, explore the world of Sinclair's *The Jungle,* and make sausage from scratch.

Unit 7: Gender, Sexuality, and the 1950s—weeks 9 and 10

- Students will be able to discuss the concepts of gender and sexuality in reference to 1950s society and make an authentic 1950s recipe.

FINAL: <u>The Louisville World Food Investigation</u>—weeks 11 and 12

- Students will be able to link the concepts of ethnocentrism, xenophobia, cultural relativism, and assimilation in exploring a specific food tradition present in Louisville while exploring the texts of the city.

Louisville World Food Investigation

Your city or town is a text that can be read in multiple ways. As Brent and I shared our food spots with each other and with students, a wide range of markets throughout the city of Louisville came into view. Most of these markets are next to a corresponding restaurant demonstrating all of the various ways to use those market-sold ingredients. We could take a global culinary tour within less than thirty minutes of driving or biking, but I had so many students telling me that Louisville was boring or that the food stunk at this particular place or that they had never bought groceries anywhere other than Walmart. With that in mind, as well as the selfish desire to have students find new restaurants and markets for me to try, the Louisville World Food Investigation was born.

We put up a laminated map of the city and did some research. Which neighborhoods are we already familiar with? Where are the gaps? What markets/

restaurants do we know about? What trends do we see? Which one should I visit? The goal was to create a compiled map of markets and restaurants in the city of Louisville complete with reviews, food selfies, and recommendations. We solved transportation problems by having students carpool or include family on the project. I also took a group to one of my favorite markets, Viet Hoa.

Students spread out all over the city, and each day we looked at the new selfies and pictures of dishes and listened to students talk about their experiences. Some students new to the United States went to Kroger and were blown away. Others more timid about stepping out of their food norms had tempura at the local sushi joint. Many students listened to their peers and visited and ate at places where other families shop and eat. A few fell in love with new flavors; all returned with a personal story about their experience, the looks they received for their hipster food photography, and questions about how that culinary tradition existed in Louisville. In addition, this project provided an invitation for the community to come into the classroom, whether as takeout, market or restaurant owners, chefs, or stories.

This project was a lot easier to execute than I thought it would be. Students placed their cards on the map (see Figure 3.2), and we started to see trends and pockets of settlement in the city. I hadn't planned it, but students used the analysis to talk about segregation, migration, social class, geography, global cuisine, and hunger, just to name a few topics. Students critiqued the project, saying that it should all be digital and passed down from class to class. Another said it should be made into a website like Yelp. I was amazed at how students so quickly began to see the city around them in a new dynamic and curious light. It was obvious to me and the students that the cultural lens can be shifted, shaped, and expanded as we experience the world around us. As an eater, I used that map to guide my culinary passions for the next year.

In teaching Environmental Studies at St. Bonaventure University, I used a similar format but in relation to environmental work. Over a summer I made a list of individuals focused on sustainability (working in a sewage treatment plant, bike store, bison ranch, solar pig farm, local brewery, etc.) and visited all of them to build a relationship. Each student then "owned" one of these institutions, reached out to them, and visited. They dug a bit deeper to do a systems analysis connecting the local work to its global impact, but the results were largely the same as those in our Louisville World Food Investigation; students saw the area around them as an interesting text to be explored, and the people in it had value and something to share. Based on the success of this project at both the university and the high school, I believe it's possible to do this in rural areas with a shift toward the expanded food system, or even to go hyper-focused and

RECIPE: _____[your city] **World Food Investigation**

Ingredients

Project: Create an expanded map of local restaurants and markets that represent the various cultures within the city, town, or county.

Ingredients
- List of restaurants and markets across a geographic area
- Phone that can take pictures
- Map of the area (laminated for repeated use)
- String, index cards, and thumbtack OR make it a digital space

Process
1. Identify restaurants and markets in the area.
2. Claim a restaurant or market that you have not been to that is off your beaten path.
3. Facilitate transportation.
4. At the location:
   a. Take a selfie.
   b. Try something new and take a picture.
   c. Find out how long the store/restaurant has been around and its history.
   d. Fill out your note card with the name of the restaurant, address, review, and any other pertinent information.
   e. Post it to the map and present it to the class.

Final Product
Annotated map of Louisville based on restaurants and markets that we all need to visit. Delish.

Map of Louisville with student project destinations.

FIGURE 3.2. Louisville World Food Investigation instructions.

have the students visit one another's homes. It's up to you to decide what community your students can explore and the learning you want to foster based on whether you are an English, history, business, sociology, journalism, geography, science . . . you get the idea . . . teacher. The text is all around you for this project.

Hunter-Gatherer Unit

The basis of our Food Sociology course is to jam food and sociology together to get students thinking and excited about studying sociology in the short term, leading to more intense academic work in the long term. The hunter-gatherer unit starts by looking at creation myths from around the world—Greek, Egyptian, Hindu, Cherokee, Semitic, scientific, Australian aborigine—including any others that are part of students' cultural heritages. From there we discuss how, in this class and in most college-level anthropology and sociology courses, the scientific creation story, which includes the big bang and the theory of evolution, is used as the basis for inquiry. Of course, this topic generates disagreements, discussions, and conversations—all of which give this class meaning.

We dive into hominids and stop at about 15,000 years ago, during the last ice age. Here we study what it means to be a hunter-gatherer, looking at pictures of Pleistocene megafauna, Clovis stone points, cave art, and archaeological sites from around the world, and debating theories about human nature, from the Marxist and the Buddhist to Hobbesian and Freudian. We become hunter-gatherers. We break up into extended family groups of three to four people and search/hunt for the bits of red, green, and brown paper I have hidden around the room to represent food. Our populations fluctuate depending on the amount of food gathered and in relation to the season, which affects food resources. We pay attention to strategy, beneficial adaptations, learned skills, and dynamics within and between the groups. It's inevitable that we start using ourselves as texts in our discussions of human nature.

Each year I track down some bison, venison, and/or elk meat. I pass it around to the kids, pointing out the muscle, bone, marrow, tendons, blood. We use a student to teach the anatomy of butchering an animal; the weirdness of that further engages the students. We place the meat in the fridge and venture out to the field in front of the greenhouse, where I have put my collection of homemade spears (rough-pointed, six-foot downed branches from behind the school) next to the straw-bale bison tied to a metal wagon with a fire of cedar wood burning in a metal bowl behind it. Each member of the family group has three spears to throw as the wagon is pulled by a fifty-foot rope; a buried spear

Senita throws.

brings food back to your family. As students throw wood at straw in the cold, they realize how huddling around fire makes people come together, and that taking down a large animal with a spear would require a massive amount of skill. They realize that the romanticized versions of the "caveman" life might be more complicated than they thought. At the same time, it's amazing to watch the students perceive the continuance of the circle as we huddle around a fire

Will launches one at the bison.

in the cold and then go back into the classroom. Some students say that sitting around in a circle talking, joking, telling stories, and singing might be hardwired into us or our culture.

With the smoke still in our hair, we prep the bison/elk/venison stew, learning basic knife skills, discussing the ingredients that would have been available before the domestication of plants and animals, praising the best hunters from the previous day, and breathing in the collective work and discussion of sociology and our shared past. Through this project-based, food-included interdisciplinary learning experience, I've had students question where sociology is still taught, wanting to study it in college, to design their own experimental archaeology experiences, to learn how to hunt, and to pursue the larger story of where we come from on theological and philosophical levels. Eating the stew literally internalizes our learning. Food becomes a link to the past that re-creates authentic physical movements that humans once shared. I can only hope to guide the bubbling-over of enthusiasm, questions, and curiosity from excited students into the next unit.

Revisionist Columbus and Pizza

Having developed a sociologist's perspective, a critical lens on the past and present, knife and dough skills, and a playful yet meaningful relationship with food, the students are ready for unit 4, "The Columbian Exchange, Genocide, and Pizza," which embraces all of that growth. We prepare students for a mock trial of Christopher Columbus by starting with the "evidence" of traditional stories and musical cartoons from the 1960s and 1970s. We add Howard Zinn's *A People's History of the United States*, primary source writings by Bartolomé de las Casas, and wood carvings by Theodor de Bry to show the depth of primary and secondary sources that shape public knowledge and perspective. With a critical lens in the circle, the class takes in these texts not as unbiased accounts but as arguments that need to be weighed and brought into concert with the dynamics, motives, and narratives that formed their existence.

We then put our new knowledge into conversation with pizza. Students learned the basics of making bread in unit 3 (see the recipe below), so now the crust becomes an assessment of recipeless dough creation. Early on the day of pizza creation, a few students come in early for a sauce lesson, and by 7:40 a.m., the hallway is heavy with the scents of basil, garlic, onion, and tomato. Then the students get creative. The toppings become an interpretation of the academic story, whether focusing on the agricultural phenomenon of the Columbian

Estefania with "syphilis" pizza.

exchange using foods from both the new and the old worlds, or on metaphors that represent revisionist history, such as using sauce and pepperoni to represent the torture and mutilation of natives. The most memorable pizza represented the exchange of syphilis; historians debate whether it was one of the diseases to go from the Americas back to Europe during this period. Syphilis pizza had a thin crust with burnt edges, tomato sauce, mozzarella, pepperoni, olives cut in half with the domes facing up, all topped with four eggs over easy. If you are wondering how that represents syphilis, Google the symptoms, use your imagination, and then translate that into high-school-speak. As the variety of deep-dish, thin, stuffed crust, and Sicilian pizzas baked with the surprise calzones, students told the story of their pizzas while their classmates' mouths watered.

As we eat the pizza, I introduce a potential bombshell of an essay, "Symbolic Racism, History, and Reality: The Real Problem with Indian Mascots" by Kimberly Roppolo. In reading this article, we try to make the connection between the histories we have been taught, our new critical lens, the author's perspective, and the pain inherent in the convergence of peoples from different parts of the world. If we weren't sitting around eating pizza we have made for one another, the class would tear itself apart. But, given these conditions, we have one of the most insightful conversations on race, discrimination, and American society I get to experience every year.

◎　◎　◎　◎

Bread as a Skill Recipe
As written on the chalkboard:

1 C lukewarm water
Spoonful of sugar, maple syrup, or honey
Spoonful of yeast
Pinch of salt
Enough flour so your hands don't stick

This is the recipe and directions I provide to students in unit 3 for making bread. I always buy a 50-lb. sack of flour. Once a group's dough ball is the right consistency and shape, they become dough checkers. Since we don't have enough time to let it rise and bake it in one period, we bag the dough in nonairtight plastic bags (like those you put produce in; Ziploc bags will explode) and place them in the refrigerator overnight. This allows a slow rise that develops gluten and flavor; if some bags overflow, students learn that they added too much yeast. With their dough, the kids make loaves, rolls, buns, baguettes, or twists, and we use two ovens, one set at a low temperature for a softer crust and one at 450 degrees with a small bowl of water for a crusty loaf.

Students are proud of their bread products and share. Some ask to take yeast and flour home, eventually bringing back photographs of their families enjoying a warm slice. By following a vague and incomplete recipe, students are forced to learn the skill of bread-making instead of practicing how to follow directions. This is essential because students need to make a crust for their pizza later on in class. You can amend the recipe by adding a spoonful of olive oil and covering the dough ball in olive oil for the nighttime rise. This adds a depth of flavor and allows the dough to stretch the next day. The same property will be seen later with the Bosnian pita recipe. But before you set a 50-lb. bag of flour and a hose in the middle of your room, make sure you have made some loaves yourself and have taken the time to build a classroom community that can handle the challenge and freedom of bread.

Questions to Chew On

1. What are the topics, standards, and lessons you have to teach that always seem like a challenge for you and your students?
2. How can you change an environmental factor in the learning experience?
3. How could you use a hands-on product as a metaphor for the targeted learning?
4. If your life were a pizza, what toppings would be on it?

Food Heritage Project

Being seen as an empty vessel that needs to be filled with knowledge must have an impact on the student mindset. It also allows for the exchange of information to be only one way, negating the ability of students to bring their significant knowledge to the class to enrich the learning environment. By the time our students get to high school, our attempts to access some of the experiential texts within each student are met with confusion: confusion that we see value in those experiences, confusion that we expect the exchange of information to flow both ways, and confusion that those aspects of life that are usually separate from school are about to become a communal text. A student's food heritage becomes the starting text to critically engage with the world of Food Lit, construct culturally sustainable identities, and openly explore the diversity within our community.

As a teacher, you must not be the most knowledgeable person in the room. You must not have all of the answers. You must be willing to accept all of the students at the table despite your own personal biases, passions, and hang-ups, food related or otherwise. This is a radical change from the traditional teacher-student relationship. In addition, a teacher interested in incorporating food into the curriculum also must have searched into their own food heritage and reflected on how that heritage has impacted them, how it represents their historical and current identity, and how to find value within the stories, ingredients, and physical actions that create a meal, dish, and tradition.

For me this process of intentionally looking deeper into my food heritage started during my early twenties after one of the many conversations with my grandfather, Paul Franzen, or as we all call him, Pop. He is the patriarch of a large (seven children) German-Catholic family that he and his now deceased wife, Lavene, raised in Roxborough, Philadelphia. Looking at the pictures of Pop when he was a medic in World War II, I could stand in as a look-alike. My father, his son, Bill, killed himself when I was thirteen. Although this was incredibly painful, that trauma changed my relationship with my grandfather. The facade, niceties, and traditions of the usual grandfather-grandson relationship fell away to the stark honesty of pain and loss, and, as I started traveling to visit my grandfather, we began speaking as two people along similar journeys, except offset by sixty-four years.

He spoke about Roxborough and how as a child he could remember a horse-drawn coal cart careening down the steep cobblestone street between the row houses toward the Schuylkill River down below. He spoke about his friends in the war, something he rarely opened up about, as his unit sailed to the north coast of Africa and worked its way up Italy, with a mix of joy in remembering and pain at the thought of those lost. I spoke about what it was like to have my mom remarry and to become the middle of seven children after being the youngest of two. I spoke about my friends and my love of being outside. I spoke about learning to work on my stepdad's farm and in his company, Liberty General Contracting.

The spark that led down the never-ending search of food heritage happened one day as Pop and I sipped Yuenglings, and he started talking about smells in the row home where he grew up in Manayunk. He remembered going down into the basement and smelling the heavy funk of fermenting cabbage, knowing that the tart taste of sauerkraut would be the result. He went on to describe the bubbling of grape must, also from the basement, and the scents from his mother's kitchen, of traditional dishes that have no written recipe but come from the hands of loved ones almost as if by instinct. When I asked him to teach me how to make these things, he said he couldn't. He had only the smells, the sights, and the tastes left; he had never learned how to cook.

I don't blame Pop, but I cringe when I think about the physical histories that defined my ancestors and know that so much of what brought them together around a table in prayer, in joy, in remembrance, in celebration, in communion, is lost. I made it my passion to reconstruct those physical and culinary histories. I bought a crock and cabbages; before long I was smelling that heavy funk of fermenting cabbage. I bought malt, barley, and hops; before long I was waiting for those first bubbles to start forming as the yeast ate sugars, just as the wine must frothed in that basement in Manayunk. My aunt, the family genealogist, shared with me a list of ingredients in a red cabbage recipe that she remembered from her childhood, with the measurements of "some," "enough," and "handfuls." In talking about experimenting with this dish, my grandfather chuckled, obviously with his head in a different time. He said that in his family they always jokingly asked the question "Is there cabbage coming out of your ears yet?" at every meal. He had forgotten that. I was making progress. I was finding out who I was, and as a result, bringing back some of the prayer, joy, remembrance, celebration, and communion that I thought was lost.

In becoming a teacher, I saw students who seemed to be floating in the miasma of messages that seek to define the identity of young people as modern consumers, independent individuals, and fully autonomous creatures who owe no debt, reverence, or respect to anything that brought them to this earth or to where they are now. Although this may sound liberating, the definition of freedom, I saw many students floundering to find identities that could sustain them, buying swampland for foundations on which to build their futures, and eschewing the relationships and structures that help to explain why they are where they are. I saw lost kids. Lost kids are vulnerable. I had found *my* answer in sauerkraut, my mother and stepdad cooking for at least seven every night of the week, McCaffrey-whiskey-soaked fruitcake, Goodyear family sticky buns. I needed to help students find their own answers through an investigation of food and to shake loose family stories in order to own recipe, story, history, and ancestry in a new way.

Some of the Goodyear Franzen-Sacks family.

◎　◎　◎　◎

Recipe: Goodyear Sticky Buns

This recipe defined Christmas morning for my brother John and me. Each year we would be sent out to our neighbors to deliver these delectable yeasty treats to the Watkins and the Werleys. Now that I've moved away and married, my mom freezes the nestled pinwheels of dough, butter, sugar, and spices before the last rising so that I can take them to my in-laws for the holiday without losing the experience of the yeast coming back to life and the plump buns being feshly baked. My wife is still working on perfecting this recipe, but I know my daughters Hazel and Eleanor will be carrying that recipe when they learn to walk.

*Doubled Recipe

Dough
⅔ C milk
½ C sugar
1 tsp salt
½ C butter
½ C warm water (appr. 115°F)
2 packages dry yeast
2 eggs
5 C all-purpose flour

In a small saucepan, heat milk until bubbles form around edge of pan. Add sugar, salt, butter, and cool to lukewarm. Sprinkle yeast on water in large bowl, stir until dissolved. Stir in milk mixture, add eggs and 2 cups flour. Beat with electric mixer until smooth. Add the rest of the flour with wooden spoon. Beat until dough is smooth and leaves the side of the bowl. Turn out dough into floured area. Knead until dough is smooth and blisters appear. Place in a greased bowl, turn to bring up greased side. Cover with towel and let rise (85° F) until doubled in bulk. (1–1.5 hours)

Filling
½ C softened butter
½ C brown sugar
1 C pecan halves
1 C chopped raisins
1 Tbsp cinnamon

Roll dough into 12" × 16" rectangle. Spread with soft butter; sprinkle with brown sugar, handful of raisins, and cinnamon, roll, pinch edge. Cut into 12 pieces; place cut side down in pan, let rise covered 1–1.5 hours. Preheat oven to 375 degrees and bake for 25–30 minutes. Invert on large cookie sheet. Let stand one minute and remove pan.

The food map introduces students to pulling at the texts within them and finding value in those stories and relationships; the Food Heritage project (FHP) challenges students to take a step further by researching, owning, preparing, and sharing a dish from their heritage. The first task, although seemingly simple, is always the most complex: find a recipe that is important to your family (ideally one that has been in the family for two generations). This activity immediately has half of the class calling relatives, which expands the texts of the class exponentially while enriching the class community. The other half is usually stuck. Figure 3.3 is the tool I have used for the FHP. It has changed a bit each year based on the research skills of the class and student input. I hand this out once students are excited about the project. If I hear any groans, I ask the groaners to choose or negotiate with me for another option. Usually these options are situationally specific and are well worth the extra conversation. My goals are to validate students' current identities using heritage as a tool and to demonstrate the multi-disciplinary methods of researching, preparing, analyzing, and presenting part of the world around us. These goals are reflected in the options in Figure 3.3. This framework can be easily tailored to an English, history, geography, home ec, health, or media studies course. Each day in class we visit the framework, which requires deeper explanation as students run into issues. Although there are gaps in the instructions, the framework provides enough flexibility to allow students to be creative and add something unique to their perspective.

The Food Heritage Project: Presented by: _____ Name of Dish: _____				
MUST:	FORM: Pick One	FAMILY: Pick One	HEALTH: Pick One	ECONOMIC: Pick One
Have full recipe with ingredients and instructions	Cooking Show Video	Documentation of cooking the dish with a relative	Analysis of caloric and nutritional values	Cost analysis of dish and per serving cost
Make the dish and bring it in*	Photo Essay	Testimonials from at least 4 family members	Rewrite a healthier version of the recipe	Analysis sourcing ingredients locally and impact
Have personal connection	PowerPoint	Family tree of relatives involved	Contextualization of dish regarding obesity, diabetes, and heart disease	Analysis of recipe reflection of socioeconomic standing
	You negotiate	You negotiate	You negotiate	You negotiate

*If there is an issue getting ingredients or cooking at home, let me know.

Potential Recipes: (Food maps can be used as a brainstorming tool.)

FIGURE 3.3. Framework for the Food Heritage project.

FHP: Conversations That Lead Home

Some students say, "I'm a normal white American." The Food Heritage project becomes an amazing opportunity to talk to students about the normalization of whiteness and that "being white" has a complex history with recipes, dishes, and unique stories. It's also an awesome time to push against the social construction of race, revisit the concept of the cultural lens, and ask them what they were before they were "just white." This conversation has led students to the delicious Welsh rarebit sandwich, German pfeffernusse cookies, handmade pasta lasagna, and a slew of other European culinary traditions that have either become Americanized or been sidelined in the past.

Some students' families have been truncated by death, adoption, lost relationships, or a host of other often incredibly painful reasons. When first implementing this project, I wasn't sufficiently prepared to respond to the needs of these students in a constructive and critical way and bumbled through the first round. I have since found a couple of strategies helpful in making this project an especially empowering experience for these students. The first is to explain how a tradition is started and becomes part of someone's heritage, and that a student without family connections is in a position to create a tradition that can be passed down, putting the student in the driver's seat of writing their own future heritage through learning a recipe and sharing it in the future. Another strategy is to reach back to an individual's larger ethnic heritage, whether that's rooted in American cuisine or in another culinary lineage, if the information is available. A turkey sausage bite grilled cheese sandwich showed me how just asking questions can lead to a solution even when the situation seems at an impasse.

One young woman, upon hearing about the project, put her head down on her desk. Once the other students were calling relatives or using their phones to look up recipes, I walked over and knelt next to her desk. She explained to me that she didn't know her father or her grandparents on either side. She lived with her mom, or, more accurately, shared an apartment with her since her mom worked second and third shifts. The student was a mix of multiple heritages but constantly felt as though she didn't belong to any of them. In addition, she said she knew eventually the dish would need to be shared and she didn't have any money. I was at a loss until I asked, "What is something you do in the kitchen that makes other people happy?"

With a sigh, she said the only thing she ever cooks is a grilled cheese for her mother. Her mom would sometimes text in the middle of the night when she was having a tough time at work, and upon waking up and seeing the message, the young woman would take two pieces of white bread, slather the outside with I Can't Believe It's Not Butter, place a Kraft single on each piece of bread, and skillfully arrange the correct amount of Hormel Turkey Sausage Bites in between the cheese, browning both sides to perfection and leaving it out for her mother, whom she would pass on her way out the door. Being in many ways a food elitist, I cringed at the mention of store-bought presliced white bread, a catchy-phrase-named butter substitute, cheese slices individually wrapped in their own cellophane, and precooked conventionally raised turkey sausage. Instead of spewing my own judgment, I told her that the level of care embodied in that sandwich demonstrates the depth of the relationship between her and her mom and that she had her recipe.

I went out and bought her the ingredients. At 6:30 a.m. she showed up to make the sandwiches since she wanted them to be perfect for her first-period classmates. I had the job of unwrapping the individual cheese slices, and we talked while we worked; I learned about her life, her mother, the intricacies of grilled cheese, college aspirations, school conflicts, and what she thought about my class. My classroom is situated across from the cafeteria, and as students arrived at school and headed to the cafeteria for breakfast, they followed their noses to our classroom. My student shot them all down, telling them authoritatively that they would not be getting a single bit of the special grilled cheese unless they were in her class. The students in our class sat and watched us cook, fling cellophane, place sausage, flip white bread, and fill the air with deliciousness. When the bell rang, the class was silent, and the young woman had her sandwiches on a platter, each sliced diagonally, just like her mother liked them.

Preparing the dish and documenting the preparation is an essential, empowering part of the project. Most important, the young woman was able to own her own recipe, find a new perspective and source of value in the relationship with her mother, define a new tradition and piece of her heritage, create community within the classroom through a shared experience that incorporated many aspects of her life that usually caused pain or weren't mentioned in the classroom, and build a personal relationship with a teacher who became her student.

FHP Makes the Classroom like Home

Documenting the dish preparation takes the class into the student's home in both a physical and a figurative manner. We have visited the kitchen of a Chinese buffet; met the best collaborative cooking team consisting of four brothers ranging from ages five to eighteen; gotten to know grandparents, parents, aunts, stepparents, brothers, sisters, numerous dogs; and seen cooking techniques that you can't find even in the glut of food- and cooking-obsessed television. Whether the dish is green eggs and ham or traditional Nepali samosas, each student respects every other student by trying the food and listening to the stories and process behind the dish as students present. Puja, who provides her recipe below, decided that a live cooking demonstration with three sous chef friends was necessary. Before I knew it, the room was filled with the enrapturing aroma of rich curry, and other students were chopping tomatoes, potatoes, and learning as the usually quiet Nepali young woman confidently ran the kitchen. That was one of many days when the smells lured people from other classes under the guise of "going to the bathroom"; the largess and pride of these young women in sharing part of themselves kept me from closing the doors. I always wondered what the other teachers thought when students returned from the bathroom licking their fingers.

Nepali Samosas—Puja B.
Preparing Dough
2¼ C self-rising flour
¾ tsp salt

6 Tbsp (¾ stick) butter, cut in small pieces
9 Tbsp pure water

Mix them all to make dough.

Take a small amount of dough and roll it with rolling pin to make a flat, circular shape. Repeat till dough ball is gone.

Preparing Curry for Dough
1½ lb well-boiled potatoes, peeling off skin. Cut into chunks.
1 C boiled "naked green mung beans"

Put 2 tsp vegetable oil in chunked potatoes and boiled green mung beans.

Medium-sized onion, chopped
1 tsp finely chopped / ground garlic
1½ tsp finely chopped / ground ginger
½ habanero minced chili
½ tsp spice blend garam masala
½ tsp turmeric powder
Cilantro, chopped

Now add 1 tsp red chili powder.

1½ tsp salt
½ juiced lemon

Mix all of that up nicely.

After you finish mixing all of these ingredients, prepare dough for the curry you just made. (See above.)

Now, wrap a spoonful or half a spoonful of curry into the small piece of rolled circular bread you just prepared. When you wrap the curry inside the bread, make sure it's triangular shaped. After you finish wrapping the bread, fill a pan halfway with vegetable oil and place it in your oven until heated through. Put 2–4 pieces of wrapped bread with curry inside into the hot oil. When you see the bread turning red, take it out and serve it.

Making Nepali samosas.

To expand the depth and interdisciplinary nature of the Food Heritage project, students can use a series of lenses to further explore their recipes. From a media studies perspective, students might create an Instagram hashtag and photo essay, a cooking video, a PowerPoint, a Prezi, a live cooking show, a cartoon, or any digital file that can be uploaded, preserved, and available to other students for future reference. Along with the actual recipe, students should include the rationale and personal connection explaining the choice of this recipe, as well as sections looking at the dish from different angles: through the eyes of a nutritionist, to investigate a healthier way to cook the dish or an evaluation of the dish in relation to diabetes, obesity, and heart disease; through the eyes of an economist, looking at the price per serving breakdown or how the dish reflects socioeconomic status in the past and present; through the eyes of a genealogist, by providing the family tree through which the recipe passed or tracing the geographic origins of the dish.

A sad consequence of a school blessed with an incredibly diverse population can sometimes be the small group of English language learners (ELL) grouped together in the corner who don't say much. Often these students feel the pressure to become Americanized socially in behavior, linguistically in learning English, and culturally in adopting the mainstream traditions of this country. As a result, sometimes these students hide from or reject their cultural heritage. Although diversity is often celebrated by superficially adding a food from another culture to a menu and ignoring the people, conflict, and history behind that food, the Food Heritage project is an invitation to bring home into the classroom on an equal footing. It encourages students to look at their heritage as a text worthy of study, practice, and sharing. The food also offers a shared language through which ELL students' parents can enter the classroom, a place that is often intimidating, a mystery, or filled with obstacles to developing relationships.

The dishes brought in by the ELL students break down an invisible barrier. The communal sharing of delicious food inevitably leads to curiosity and questions: "What did you call this?" "What language is that?" "Where is this from?" "Can I go there?" It leads to sharing language and the landscape of our identities. It leads to pride in what one experiences as normal. It leads to laughing together and accidentally bumping hands as students reach for the same serving spoons. Unseen barriers come down. After this project, I have seen a marked difference in where people sit in class, who people talk to, how groups work together, and, especially important for a social sciences class, more confident individuals who will share their life experiences from around the world, improving the education and perspective of the class as a whole.

As a person who has had to revive family recipes from the past or with the help of grandpa Google, the most important aspect of the FHP is that the students experience the same physical sensations that someone in their past experienced. This can be the texture of the dough in making sticky buns as you knead them. It can be the smell of sautéing onions that make the tears in your eyes worth it. It might be in developing the technique for pinching the dumpling wrapper after putting in the perfect amount of filling. It's the feel, the smells, the tastes, and especially the emotions when you put something on the table that is such a part of you—and the host of people who helped create who you are—for other classmates who are going through the same process, as well as watching others enjoy it. Students come away from this project proud of who they are, encouraged to test out new skills in the kitchen, cook for others, explore the food of other cultures, and respect individuals as part of the class community, and with a greater insight into how food can be a text within us that has the potential to connect with everyone and everything on the outside. The way I know this to be true is that at the end of every FHP cycle, as well as at the end of every student's dish presentation, we sit in the circle and reflect on what we did. Familiar with the expectations of the class by this point, students go deep, engaging in a meaningful intersection of food, identity, and community while pushing one another to elaborate on where the experience could take them.

As I refined this project, I found many authors who offered insight and an expanded perspective on researching food heritage. These also provided me with the ability to counter the "I don't have culture/heritage; I'm just _____." In that counter is the empowerment of that student. *Cuisine and Culture: A History of Food and People* by Linda Civitello, *An Edible History of Humanity* by Tom Standage, and *High on the Hog: A Culinary Journey from Africa to America* by Jessica B. Harris all provided me with foundational knowledge for this project. However, the field of food writing has exploded, offering cookbooks, narratives, and histories of many cuisines and traditions and would offer any educator interested in taking on this project a foundational perspective from which to start.

Food Heritage Project Reflection: Doughnuts (Elizabeth C.)

Saturday mornings in my house feels like a Monday. My day consists of tedious hours of cleaning. Even with the habitual routine, the house does not stay clean for more than three days and if I dare complain, my mom would recite her favorite ringtone. *"What you are doing here is nothing compared to what I did in Liberia. At the age of eleven, I took it upon myself to sell doughnuts to help my mom pay for my school fees. If you were still in Africa, you would be happy to do this small work. I don't ask you to do much, I woke up every morning at three to prepare the dough. Around five, I fried the doughnuts, took it on the road, and made sure the pan was empty before I came home. I would get done selling around noon and prepare for afternoon school."*

Elizabeth's Liberian doughnuts.

When the Food Heritage Project (FHP) was introduced in Mr. Franzen's Food Sociology class, I recalled my mom's rants and decided on the recipe. I intended to mimic the routine she explained to prove that it was all exaggeration. Apart from my scheme, the sugar coated doughnuts are scrumptious and I hadn't eaten them in a while. I set my alarm to 3:00 am the night before to ensure an accurate plan. Yawns and nods advanced concurrently during the dough process. Since I was not used to waking up that early, I took a cat nap as the dough rose. I got up some minutes to five to shape and fry the doughnuts. Thoughts about the facility I have came to mind when I fried the doughnuts. My mom probably had to wait a few minutes for the wood to catch fire while this stove heats up in seconds. My epiphany proved my mom to be right. As a student, I couldn't imagine applying that to my morning procedure. She worked harder than I ever did to get a decent education. . . . Complaining is not an option for me because being in America is a privilege. I have the opportunity to become who I want to be.

After being in America for ten years, I've assimilated to the culture so people assume I'm only American. The food heritage project gave me an opportunity to share a part of me that would not have been revealed to my classmates within the twelve week course. During the trimester, I did not interact with others or participate in discussions. This was mainly because I was new to the school and found talking difficult. The FHP is a symbol of breaking out of my shell and revealing my background. The day I presented my food, I heard people who I don't normally talk to call my name and compliment my dish. I remember Mr. Franzen asked if my mom was proud of me. My answer was yes because I took an interest in her life and extended it by creating a momentary experience to understand her struggle. I'm not normally in the kitchen with my mom, but I was during the entire project delighted with myself. I was pleased to share a taste of my home to the class. Now they don't know me as the quiet girl but the quiet Liberian girl named Elizabeth.

Long-Term Projects

High schoolers are often seen as apathetic. A lot of them are, and most of the time it is our fault. When learning is prescriptive and knowledge is held by a sage on the stage, most students define learning as something they can't do without a paid adult in the room telling them what to do and think. In addition to living this limiting perspective of what learning can be, modern teenagers have every possible distraction on the handheld computer in their pockets: games, popularity contests, porn, celebrities, material goods, and every combination thereof. Sometimes it seems like the only thing teenagers aren't apathetic about is being able to use their phones and having access to wifi. This situation, which has largely come about during my tenure as a teacher, has made teaching a lot harder. Many veteran teachers tell me they would now advise any young person to steer clear of teaching as a profession.

What the long-term project (LTP) tries to do is be an aid to curiosity, self-directed learning, and student empowerment. After the first unit, in which the students have built a class community and started to understand how I run a classroom, I introduce this project. The students can choose whatever topic and project they want as long as they see it as addressing a problem their community faces. While in the circle, we brainstorm these challenges and potential solutions without critique or shooting down ideas. I go over the schedule with three checkpoints and model how to set goals and develop a game plan, and I let them know they can depend on being able to devote a class period per week to the project. They have a week to develop a plan A Big Hairy Audacious Goal (BHAG), a plan B if A fails, and a plan C that can be accomplished if everything else goes wrong. If a students gets stuck, we go back to the circle or hold small-group conferences. About 90 percent of students will have their plans done by the end of that week and are excited to get started. I give them the time, space, and support to get going. I also give them the trust they need to collaborate, visit teachers, call professionals, and send out emails with my endorsement.

The other 10 percent usually have been in educational realities where classrooms were on intellectual lockdown, where the link between curiosity, passion, and school has been severely traumatized. Many of these 10 percenters struggle with grades and attendance and are the most difficult to engage in a class beyond compliance. I spend a lot of time with these students asking them what they care about in life, what makes them upset, what their dream jobs would be, what they think is unjust in the world. We come up with multiple plans and work to lay them out step by step. Encouraging them, reassuring them that their idea isn't dumb and that they can do something meaningful is a constant challenge throughout the process. It makes me wonder how many times the educational system has let them know they should see themselves as dumb and powerless. For students who continue to struggle to develop a project out of their own passion after that scaffolding, I provide guidance in joining an ongoing project such as rebuilding the school's watershed by planting trees, constructing benches for the mobile outdoor classroom, or adding to the garden mural.

I set aside one period a week for students to work on their long-term projects. I make myself available for conferencing and have Google Chromebooks on hand for students to use. By the second work period, students usually are rolling on their own; my job begins to emulate the little boy in 1800s paintings trying to keep the hoop rolling with his little stick. When the hoop hits a rock, I demonstrate different ways to deal with obstacles and setbacks. When we realize the hoop we're trying to control is fifty feet tall, I work with the student to scale down the project. The check-ins are half sheets with probing questions such as "What did you accomplish this week?" "How did it contribute to the larger goal of the LTP?" "What are the obstacles you encountered and what solutions have you found?" What are the next steps?" How can I support you in that next step?" Also on the sheet is the mandatory explanation of the "gist." The reiteration of the gist is designed to help students develop the skill to give an elevator pitch about their project, create the confidence and language to present at the end of the term, and explain to administration why they are out of class

The farm came to the Creek as part of Dallis's long-term project.

doing all sorts of activities. Halfway through the term, we set our presentation dates. For those who are slacking without me noticing, this often is the prod to get things rocking.

Two-thirds of the way through the trimester, students start presenting, whether due to their speedy work, anxiety, or timing. For one of these LTPs, two young men, a volunteer firefighter and a budding outdoorsman, developed and taught a fire safety lesson to the class. It consisted of a PowerPoint, a short film, a Q&A, and a fire demonstration. They taught us how to protect ourselves and also how to manage a fire. As a class, we lit a campfire and made s'mores. Once we all had chocolate and marshmallow on our faces, they showed us how to safely put out a fire, and as we did so, we talked about the fire set by two teenagers that had recently swept through the Smokey Mountains. Once back in class, we graded the students. We asked whether their work served to help a larger problem in their community. We asked whether they were engaging and informative. We assessed what we had learned. For the students who hadn't yet presented, this evaluation empowered them to take a new look at their work and be able to self-assess.

For long-term projects, I have had students learn how to grow hot peppers to make their own salsa. Others mapped the trees on campus and made a Learning Forest Walk. Two young men developed a class basketball bracket; we all came together to play the game, some of us stepping outside of our comfort zones and strengthening our communities. Other students have interviewed ELL students about their experiences at the school, both culturally and in relation to discrimination. Some students have planned and prepared traditional meals from home for the class. Others documented service work they do to share and show the good things people in the class are doing that others might not know about. A trio brought in the chief of the Louisville Metro Police Department for a conversation with the Global Issues classes. Another taught us about Japanese rock and roll culture.

We have had chicken coops, picnic benches, garden beds, birdhouses, and bat houses built. A young woman wanted students to make the connection between the meat on their plates and live animals. She invited a local farmer to class who, to my surprise, brought in a horse, a calf, a ram, ducks, rabbits, goats, and a milking cow. About half of the school made an appearance as word of the project made the rounds. The student was empowered and made at least ten new vegetarians that day. Students have mounted food drives and campus cleanups and spent hours with our Functional Mental Disability (FMD) classes to support learning and community integration. Students have written letters to politicians, administrators, and teachers.

Do all of these projects have an amazing finish? Not really. Some students (5 percent at most) give a short, unenthusiastic presentation that shows little curiosity or passion. I always feel bad about not being able to rebuild that connection between passion and learning for the student. They do, however, see the other projects where that connection was either remade or strengthened. As a class at the end of these projects, we stand in awe as we compile all of the work that has been done and the collective impact it has made in the community.

The coolest part of these projects is running into students who have graduated and moved on. They remember their project and can clearly recall how it made them feel empowered and shaped the path of their current work and learning. After hearing these accounts, I am left wondering what happens when apathetic teenagers who don't reconnect curiosity, passion, and learning become adults.

Tips for Implementing an LTP

It took four years of students participating in Food Lit, Global Issues, Food Sociology, and Cooking Club before we attracted enough students to offer a class like Global Issues Advanced and the long-term project. Those classes and experiences empowered students, built community and inherent accountability, established trust, and demonstrated to students that learning was exciting and in their hands. Without those layers of Panzenland, circle discussions, cooking together, huddling around a campfire in the cold, and the various situations that forced us to know one another in an authentic manner, these projects would have been failures and we wouldn't have had the freedom needed to execute them. However, getting your class ready to take on LTPs doesn't need to start with a pancake breakfast to build community; it could be a ropes course, a campus cleanup, a mentoring program, a camping trip . . . something that encourages students to look at themselves as part of a community they have ownership of. Developing those layers of relationship is essential to doing work that matters, as is encouraging the mindset that the world is up for grabs and investigation.

When you start an LTP, you will have failures. Some students will need lots of support and others won't. Some students will thrive in the freedom and others will procrastinate or take advantage of the space. You will have to adjust the documentation requirements to match your students and your goals for the class. Planning and accountability are essential for both you and the student. If either side drops the ball, the project can slide.

Understand that sometimes what a student sees as a community need may not match what you see. Provide space for group and individual conversations. Also understand that some of these projects will teach you and introduce you to ideas and situations you could never have imagined when you started teaching—such as managing a petting zoo for a thousand students or getting schooled on the basketball court while wearing hiking boots. Most important, though, laugh and have fun with the students as they fail and celebrate when they win.

Compassion + Cooking: A Long-Term Project (Emily R.)

"What the hell is an English Lab and who the hell is Brent Peters?", I asked myself walking towards my second period class of sophomore year after double-checking my schedule to make sure it actually said what I thought I read. I thought I knew exactly what sophomore year of high school was going to include: getting my permit, going to games, and joining as many clubs as possible. But this class in my schedule was a curveball; the juniors had no idea who this person was, much less any of us sophomores. With a million questions running through my head, I was lucky to have caught myself before I ran into the line outside my new 2nd period classroom.

"What in the world . . . ?" I'd never stood in line to enter a class before. As I gradually neared the door, I noticed a tall, somewhat lanky man in an apron greeting his students one by one, shaking their hands with intense eye contact. Growing up in a family of teachers I thought I had met every type of teacher; in that moment, I realized I hadn't. I knew I'd be venturing into new territory, something I was uneasy about.

"Good morning!" said Mr. Peters, with firm handshake, "and your name is . . . ?"

"Emily, sir."

"Welcome! Take a seat please, I'm glad you're here!"

It took me a minute to process having an actual interaction with my teacher on the first day (How sad is that?).

Finally the bell rang, signaling class to begin. Out of the corner of my eye, I see Mr. Peters awkwardly half run, half walk to the front of the classroom. He pressed a button on his laptop, opening a PowerPoint and looks up at us and exclaims, eyes twinkling, "Welcome to Food Literacy!"

Prior to this, I grew up in the kitchen. My great grandmother watched me during the day while my mother was at work from the time I was a newborn until I went to kindergarten. She did NOT believe in going out to eat; it costs too much money, and she could fix the same things at home. She cooked three meals a day, seven days a week, and usually I was there for all three. She also made homemade sourdough bread and waffles from her own starter weekly. From the time I could stand up and use a spoon, I was her sous chef. She was the first person to teach me how to use a knife, why flour should be sifted, and so much more. After I had started school, I would finish homework in her kitchen, and we would usually bake something. When my mom started graduate school, dinner was often left up to me, allowing me to experiment and explore the kitchen on my own. By the time I got to Peters and Franzen, I'd clocked more hours in the kitchen than most adults. I just hadn't been able to express my talent at school before; it had been isolated to my home life.

Food Lit provided me with an opportunity to bridge the gap between my life at home and my life at school. Peters invited me to Cooking Club on Wednesday afternoons every week after school. It soon became the unwind point of my week. I finally got to show off and wow my peers with a previously hidden talent, and I got to connect with others who shared the same talent (or sometimes un-talent) and passion for food that I did. I found my niche in the school. During senior year, I was granted an opportunity to use my talent to improve lives in my community. In our Advanced Global Issues class, Franzen presented us with the opportunity to start businesses within the school and he suggested I start a catering company. I started drafting out how that might work, retweaked it, and came up with a dinner service called Dinner by the Creek. On Monday I would send out a menu to the faculty, they would reply with their orders by Tuesday afternoon, and Friday afternoon orders were ready for pick-up/delivery. I'd prep on Wednesday, cook on Thursday, and finalize orders on Friday (at the latest). This all happened during the class periods I had with Franzen. All the profits from [the] company went back into the Cooking Club, keeping it well funded all year. Over the course of the year, I made dishes such as Chicken Cacciatore, Seafood Scampi, Vegetable Lo Mein, and other high quality dinners from various cuisines. By the end, I had an outstanding reputation of serving "5-star restaurant" quality foods.

What inspired me to start this and keep this going was growing up with a mom who is a teacher. Before she went to graduate school, we had family dinners about every night. While she was getting her degree, most nights she was in class or doing homework, so dinner got left up to take out, frozen meals, or on a rare occasion up to me. I remember eating a lot of Chinese and DiGiorno pizza. Once she graduated and started teaching, she'd come home exhausted or overloaded with papers to grade, resulting in the same kinds of dinners. At Fern Creek, we had several first year teachers, teachers with families, and teachers getting their Master's degrees. I saw my mom in these hard working teachers. I knew what their families were going through and the stress it was putting on their home lives and relationships. I wanted to ease some of that burden, even if it was only once a week. And it turned out I got the response I wanted. Returning customers would pass on rave reviews from their families and loved ones they got to sit down and enjoy their dinners with. No matter how frustrating or challenging keeping the service going was, receiving those reviews from happy loved ones the following week kept me going. I was making a difference in the lives of teachers' families, the life I went home to after school.

A year later: This service no longer exists. In the school, there was no one to pass it on to. The person I thought could handle it went on a different pathway. I heard when I left, everyone kept bugging Franzen about when it was coming back, which shows the impact it had. When I came back to visit, I stopped by some of the teachers that regularly ordered and here's some of the feedback I got:

> This was one of my favorite programs run through our school. Food is something that contributes to culture in so many ways, and it was amazing to see students planning, executing, and delivering meals week to week. When I told teachers from other schools about it they were instantly jealous. We used to joke that without this program we really would be starving artists!
>
> —Courtney Williams, Art Teacher

> At the beginning of the school year, I was new to Fern Creek and trying to involve myself in as many things as possible to get to know students outside of class. When I learned of Emily's small business, I was interested in supporting her, but also getting to know her as a person. What I found was that I got more than a meal once every week. I discovered the passion Emily had for providing a meal to others, and her dedication to making the meal options nutritious and delicious. But more importantly I found that I had more precious time at home with my family.
>
> —Lauren Niemann, Science Teacher

> The soup was out of control good! Loved it. Also, glad the cornbread was not sweet. That is the real way in KY. Otherwise, we call it cake.
>
> —Karen Morris, English Teacher

Family dinners became a huge part of these families' lives, that service gave them something back: time. As a chef, knowing the demand for my food is wonderful. But on a larger scale, I realized I gave my customers time. There was no extra stop between work and home to grab dinner and there was no prep and cook time fixing dinner. Whatever time [was] lost in logistics was given back to them. That's what means the most to me as an entrepreneur. Personally, when I moved away I didn't have the resources to keep it going. I could've figured out a space and funding to start it up, but there wasn't a market for it. I thought I was

Peters, Quentin, and Rainbolt prepare roasted cauliflower BBQ sandwiches on pretzel buns for teacher professional development. This recipe and Rainbolt made it into the local paper.

a nobody freshman [in college] who didn't have the network to build a company out there. Plus I wasn't planning on staying long. Now that I think about it, I might've been able to pull it off, but hindsight is 20/20. I've had little voices in my head telling me to start it up again as an independent company.

Where does the capacity to do these things reside? Is it in you, me, the community . . . ? It would be foolish to say that the capacity resided in me alone. My determination and willpower helped a lot but I couldn't have done it without the support of a community. Teachers could have easily turned their noses up on the idea of a student cooking them dinner or administration could've shut it down on the grounds of sanitation or the risk of a private party making a profit off the school. But they didn't; they provided an environment of support that allowed me to spread my wings and kick some ass.

What happened in that class isn't happening in other classrooms in America. Growing up with a mom and grandmother who were teachers and teacher assistants, I've been in a lot of classrooms. What made these classes different was the open line of communication, trust, and willingness for risk. These classrooms ran on the idea, "It's better to ask for forgiveness than to ask for permission," and that ended up working really well because it opened a lot of doors [that] wouldn't have been open otherwise. A lot of potential remains hidden because of the stigma placed on risk by the powers above the classroom and the world outside of it. But in all honesty, anyone in the educational system [is] scrutinized no matter what decision they make so they may as well do what they think is best and do the cool thing rather than play it safe and be scrutinized for nothing. Personally, I'd rather be yelled at for something I did and felt like it had a purpose rather than taking the safe route and feeling like it didn't mean anything in the long run. So what happened in Food Lit was Franzen and Peters took the risk and trusted their kids to take off with the opportunity they opened up. They tapped into hidden potential by believing in us before we believed in ourselves. As corny as that sounds, it's not common practice to have faith in students and the difference it makes is astounding.

Desire to Inspire: High School as an LTP (Quentin S.)

A mind is a terrible thing to waste, but an inspired mind is impossible to waste. No matter the assignment, no matter the school, no matter the job: Inspiration is the key to success. As owner of the Baxter Avenue Morgue* in Louisville, Kentucky, one of the most highly respected haunted attractions in the tri state (Indiana, Kentucky, and Ohio) area, both for customers and actors, I find myself working with anywhere from 20 to 40 new actors a season. The similarities between the two, the classroom and Morgue, never cease to end. I practically become a teacher, as most new actors have never worked at a haunted house and sometimes have never even been to one. With a whole industry to explain to a large group of people, I have found Inspiration to be one of the most successful tools for reaching out to my actors and also one of the best tools used by Joe and Brent to engage me in high school. When facing 30+ kids at the beginning of a class it may seem like it will be an uphill battle to get any work done, however, the amazing multi-tool of inspiration is in your tool box. Before

Quentin S., FCHS class of 2016, haunted house owner and operator, inventor, entrepreneur.

---

*In 2015, Quentin and his sister bought the family haunted house business, Baxter Avenue Morgue.

you can dive into inspiring the strangers that face you in your classroom, you must get to know them. Becoming better acquainted with your students is the first stone of the foundation of any effective and efficient classroom.

Without talking to my employees on a personal level and getting to know them, it would be impossible for me to know how to work with them, what to expect to receive from them in terms of quality of work and even how to interact with them. Establishing a personal connection to each of your students is vital if you expect to lead an effective and meaningful classroom. There is an inherent feeling of being less than the teacher when a student enters a class. This again resembles the way an employee views a boss. When a student or employee feels that they are on the bottom of the chain of command, it tends to be hard for them to do anything but the bare minimum. The establishment of a personal connection works to destroy this disparity between the teacher and student. In a way, a student has to be shown that their teacher is human, or else the disconnect between the two will corrode the environment of the classroom. Let your classroom know about yourself, but also get to know your students. Whether

Cedar Aldo Leopold Benches made by Quentin for a Cane Run Elementary outdoor classroom.

it's asking about students' weekends just as Brent Peters did with every student in Food Literature my entire sophomore year at Fern Creek; or simply being a human, making mistakes, and showing your students that you are not perfect. One of my fondest memories of breaking the feeling of disparity between a teacher and myself was simply a mistake Joe made one day after school. After a full trimester of Joe Franzen telling me and the other garden workers to wear gloves and goggles before even getting near a saw, I saw Joe Franzen cut his hand while sawing a PVC pipe while glove- and goggle-less. It was one of the last times I saw him more as a teacher than a friend.

Actions like that are the best answers to the age old question that is ingrained in the high-schoolers mind *"but when am I actually going to use this?"* After that day I was the one chasing students around telling them to put gloves on. When you can see through the eyes of your teacher, it is a lot easier to learn a lesson.

After seeing that Joe and Brent cared about us, it changed my whole perception of school. Every student is different, and it may take time to get to know them but in the long run the connection will aid every student in immeasurable ways. When a student sees that their teacher genuinely cares for their students it becomes a lot easier to learn from them. While the connection helps the students learn, it will also help the teacher to trust his or her students. For Joe to trust our class to start fires, use power tools, explore our school in a different light by talking to administration and our teachers, speak in public, and even run to Lowe's to buy garden supplies with the money we made selling eggs, he had to get to know us first. With each student being so different, by getting to know us he could know who to trust, who needs help and who can help others. In a classroom with no trust the opportunities that you give your students are a complete gamble. But when you close the gap between your students, get to know their abilities and limits, the odds will always be in your favor.

It is also imperative to have meaningful and interesting lesson plans and activities. When students know that they receive one worksheet during class and one for homework every day, they tend to lose interest in the class fairly quickly, while also losing interest in the teacher. It is just as boring for students to work on worksheets every single day, which they know will never amount to anything. One of my biggest allegories that I used in my portion of our presentation at The National Council of Teachers of English Convention in Washington, DC (another amazing opportunity that Joe and Brent helped Savannah, Richard, Kaila, Estephania, and myself take part in) happened one day while cleaning out the feces-filled chicken coops. I realized that the shredded paper from the offices at Fern Creek we used to fill up the clean chicken nests were graded worksheets, signed papers, and school projects. As long as I can remember working in the garden, the office had been giving us these shredded papers. And that's when I began to imagine how much time, resources, work, and thought went into what eventually soaked up chicken shit. All of those people's time and work wasted, and with nothing to show for it. But using this story helped me show the teachers we presented to that there are better ways of handling students time and work, instead of squandering everyone's unique talents by letting all the students efforts end up on paper that will be fed into the shredder. Every student's and teacher's time and effort can be harnessed leading to an environment where no one's talent or energy goes to waste. If all of that work had been harnessed in a constructive and positive way, like the garden, cooking club, or creative writing club, imagine what would have been accomplished! By throwing in meaningful, interesting, and constructive assignments that students can actually see amounting to some sort of importance they are more likely to put more work into the class, respect you more, and break down the disconnect between school and home life. In addition, when students know that you put work into their assignments they begin to see you as a friend.

This level of friendship is reciprocal. When students know that you care about them, and their daily activities, they begin to care about you too. On more than one occasion we would be in the garden and someone would start to get crazy and someone would interrupt with *"if you* [get hurt, get caught, mess up] *we are gonna lose Joe's trust."* Students recognize when they are given respect and special opportunities, and the last thing they want to do is lose either. In Global Issues advanced when the construction team would be outside, the feeling of *"how can we not get caught?"* magically became *"how can we do this right, and show the school this is what class should be like?"* Without Joe trusting us, there is no telling the trouble we would have gotten into. But, that trust was contingent on him getting to know us, and becoming our friends. Once there are no more strangers in your classroom, you can begin to inspire.

Inspiration is the driving force behind a functional and efficient classroom. The current Education System in America is designed to process and not to produce—an inefficient machine that simply takes raw materials in and breaks them down even further. Again, all those assignments that took anywhere from an hour to a week for students to fill out end up nowhere, cluttering teachers' desks, shredded, trashed, or best case scenario covered in chicken feces. But we keep this inefficient and ineffective system running because, "Hey, they pass those standards, so they must be getting *something* out of all this". The current model aims to minimize expression on the student's part. After all, it is a lot easier to run a machine if every part you stick into it has the same size, shape, and ideas. If you worry too much about how every student is going to strictly adhere to all of the little things like dress code, hallpasses, 10 minute lunches, and all the other redundancies that so many schools have set in place, you end up with students that never learn a single thing throughout high school beside how to get around all of the stupid little rules that beat students into submission to make them easier for the machine to process. Students end up tired of fighting, and eventually lose all traces of individuality. And without being themselves, how are students ever expected to get anything done?

Inspiration is the multi-tool that must be used to fix up the derelict machine that is high-school education, and make the switch from processing mindless zombies to producing actual citizens, capable of life outside a controlled environment. The key to inspiring your students is to let them be themselves. Again, getting to know your students greatly helps the disconnect of teacher and student, but it also greatly reduces the disconnect of students home life and school life. When students don't have to become a different person everyday for school, they are able to become a lot more comfortable with school. When students can't be themselves, they end up not wanting to put any work forward, especially because students know that if all the work is [the] same, that someone is bound to do it, and *"why would I do the work when I can just copy from someone else?"* This is why it is so vital for teachers to design their students assignments on an individual basis. How can you cheat or cut corners on a completely self directed assignment?

In Food Literature, Curiosity + Challenge was a perfect example of a completely self directed project where students could be themselves. Over winter break students were asked to design a project and set a goal for themselves and record their progress. The project was completely self directed and the documentation was to be presented when school was back in session. Students chose an astounding variety of topics, from solving severe community issues like homelessness or hunger all the way to reading the entire Harry Potter series. But in every student's case, the outcome was the same. Students got excited about bringing something they care about from their home-life to school, and offer it to be measured in a meaningful way. For the first time many students saw that there doesn't have to be a disparity between reality and school.

In advanced Global Issues, the overall goal of the class was to pick a problem the world faces and to solve that issue in an innovative way on a local level. Like Curiosity + Challenge, this helped to bring students lives into the classroom yet again. By seeing their personal lives in school, students became inspired to do more than just the minimum. It is extremely hard to get excited about something that you have no connection to. However, when students saw that they were able to use school as a tool to solve a problem that plagues their society, it became more than just school, more than standards and homework, more than the bare minimum they had to put forth every day. Class became a way to accomplish something, to be a part of something bigger than one person's needs

The Global Issues Adv. construction crew posing on the half-completed outdoor kitchen.

or wants. Even those students that had no idea what was important to them became aware of the problems around them, and were inspired to make a difference in their own lives. One student raised over 300 lbs. of food in the form of a food drive to give to those who go without; another started a team to compost food waste in the cafeteria to reduce the environmental impact of the school. Again, this was completely self directed, and students used their own lives to become inspired in school. My Project started out in Global Issues I to build a windmill to help power the garden; however, because of administration limiting the height we could build to, I instead built a bicycle powered generator that we eventually ended up taking to present to Prince Charles and the Duchess of Cornwall while they visited Louisville. I built it from a spare alternator from my first car, a 1970 Ford LTD, [and] angle iron I found in the rafters at the Morgue, a bike that a teacher had donated after Joe sent out a faculty e-mail, and spare wood and paint from the garden. The generator was a model to show how it was difficult, but possible to derive power from sustainable sources. I was able to build this generator thanks to the freedom that Joe gave me in Global issues.

In both of these classes, with both of these projects many students found ways in which they could break down the disparity between home and school. These opportunities are extremely rare after grade school, and the idea of bringing your home life to school often seems taboo to students. However, looking back on our time with Joe and Brent, I realize that times we spent feeling like school was our home were undoubtedly the most valuable of our high school career. The dedication it took on their part was immense, but it eventually paid off in so many ways. If there was one thing I could pass onto teachers, it would be to never stop inspiring. The inspiration derived from Food Lit and Global Issues I & II could be traced all over the school, state, and nation. I know for sure that my inspiration physically took me all the way to Washington D.C. for NCTE, and mentally put me on another planet. It is not always about putting a ton of work into a class for it to be successful, but instead just putting enough to inspire your students to take themselves further than any class ever could. I was able to solidify all of my hard work into the garden, with my generator, and by building two whole 10′×10′ chicken coops, one a modern-looking passive solar structure. The other, a more traditional rustic, completely recycled coop with a 10′×20′ pavilion (also completely recycled) attached. The latter of the two really is my standing achievement of senior year. Joe let me completely design and build it with other student in Advanced Global Issues. We were able to use earth packed tires for the foundation, tree trunks for the pavillon supports, and aluminium mesh table tops covered with old billboards for the roof. Inspiration leads us down our own channels, and for me because of Joe and Brent my inspiration didn't end up in a paper shredder, or in the garbage; my energy was solidified in those coops and will always be there. It all just depends on how you harness your time and energy, and inspiration.

Recipe: Truck-Cycle—Quentin S.
Ingredients:
1 tandem style bike
1 pallet's worth of wood (sanded and pulled apart)
a ton of bike chain
3 milk crates
multiple miscellaneous metal pipes
1 3′ section flat iron or similar material
. . . and a lot of patience.

Instructions:
The truck-cycle is a bike I built senior year as a way to get to the garden without driving, but also giving me enough space to bring produce and water back and

forth. I made my truck bed big enough to fit 3 milk crates in, which I found in the school's trash. I started with a 1971 Sears Sportflite model tandem style bike frame that I actually bought, but the tandem frames can be easily made with a welder and a little bit of patience. My love for bikes almost surpases that of the Morgue, so the truck cycle is a good representation of my home life mixing with school life.

*To find a tandem bike, I recommend second-hand stores or building one. Beg, cheat, or steal, you have to acquire one for this recipe. Also, they get better with age.

- Get it Running! You can't cook with unripe fruits or vegetables, and you can't build a bike if you can't ride it. I had to replace the tires and tubes on mine, and put new chains on it. Do whatever it takes!

- Remove the passenger seat and handlebars. It just so happened that mine came with some sick ape-hanger style bars that I upgraded to the driver's seat.

- Build your truck bed. Just like cooking a dish, this takes a lot of work on the chef or builders part. This is a lot of eyeballing, trial and error, and the builders opinions. Sometimes you have to add ingredients until it tastes or fits just right.

- Once you've got your bed built, use the now empty passenger's seat tube to mount your bed to the bike; since seat tubes are angled, this might throw you a curveball. I found it was easy to use a level to mark the tube to cut it flush. Attaching your bed to the seat tube can be tackled thousands of different ways. I chose to weld a piece of flat steel to the tube and this allowed me to screw the tube directly to the bed. Attach your seat tube to your bed in any way that you can with the tools that you have.

- Use some flat iron to make brackets that run from the right rear corners of the bed to the axle of the rear wheel. Bolt the bottom of these brackets on in the same way you would a fender or de-railer. Screw or bolt the top of these brackets straight to the bed. Make them as strong as possible.

- Thoroughly ride for a whole summer, water jug and produce bungeed down for each trip back and forth. Solve any issues that arise on the road, and when it becomes a trusty ride stick a fork in it, it's done!

Finished truck-cycle ready to haul veggies.

◎　◎　◎　◎

Student Editing: Long-Term Project (Trey H.)

Another opportunity provided by Food Lit. was becoming a student editor for *Tigers Feeding Chickens* [*Tigers Feeding Chickens* was the original title of *Say Yes to Pears*]. In January of 2016, Mr. Franzen offered me a space in his newest class, Global Issues Advanced, one with no formal structure. His third trimester, fourth period students were split into groups dedicated to the garden, the local environment, the book, or the catering company. We didn't have someone leering over our shoulders. We didn't have any essays or tests. Our only motivation was to do well for the sake of our projects and show Franzen his trust had not been misplaced.

That is not to say that Mr. Franzen disappeared; he was always around for lunch period to answer questions and update groups on extra work to be done. He just wasn't going to constantly chase us down to force us into work, we were trusted to be responsible students. That is why I, a senior in high school at the time, was allowed to be one of the first editors to Peters and Franzen's book.

As the above sentence hints, I'm still just a student. I have no degree in English. I've never edited for anything that was meant to be published besides a high school literary magazine. I'm just a kid that got the first shot at editing a book meant to teach teachers. Editing the book was a ton of fun and opened my eyes to a potential career path.

Both the trust and freedom the course offered were very reminiscent of Curiosity + Challenge, just on a much larger scale and with a bit less choice in project. At the end of twelve weeks the group I was assigned had edited and formatted the book (what there was of it at least), conducted interviews of Food Literacy students, and documented our own experiences with the program. For twelve weeks I was responsible for my own work and what I learned, and it was one of the most enriching experiences of my high school career.

To back up that statement, I have more than words. To start there's the binder with the original print out of *Tigers Feeding Chickens,* the first version of Chapter 1 my group was handed on the first day. We spent the entire first week passing the sections around, annotating them, discussing and planning out changes. That was when I took over as the head of the group concerning editing, organizing who checked what and approving changes to be brought to Franzen's attention. Next, we moved to Google Docs to actually begin piecing together the chapter. At that point we were also given the task of conducting a series of interviews on Food Maps; so, to complete all of our work, I was given the sole job of formatting the document.

It was an odd experience; Mr. Franzen and Mr. Peters treated me as an equal as we all edited the document. This was especially visible as the final changes were being made; the three of us brainstormed names for sections through text messages during spring break. All through the process of editing, formatting, editing again, and adding to the chapter none of my ideas or critiques were disregarded just because I was a student. If something wasn't changed or implemented it was because something better was come up with or the original fit better with the chapter as a whole; either way I was taken seriously. That's a rare experience, even in classes where the teachers try to treat their students like adults; how many would trust a student to edit and format a section of anything they planned to publish, let alone an entire chapter? Franzen and Peters trusted Sharada, Ariel, Muslima and I though. That trust earned all of us students experience in a possible job; we could all go to college and decide to become editors and having worked closely with the two authors of an educational book as high schoolers will look nice on any resume. Peters and Franzen got to see how other people viewed what they wrote, and had access to people who have gone through their classes to point out any details they missed.

The class hasn't just taught me about editing either; no, I learned a very important lesson about long term group work. You don't necessarily have to like each other to get all the work done. Now, that doesn't mean my group mates and I hate each other or are even on bad terms. Specifically Sharada, leader of all interview projects, and my personalities do not smoothly mesh. At first we argued, quite a few times, but eventually we all realized a) we cannot get anything done like this, b) it doesn't take four people to conduct an interview, and c) we're good at different things. So, we divided and conquered: Sharada and the others would conduct interviews while I edited, and on days that editing was marked as a priority Ariel would stay with me to help while Sharada scheduled interviews for later and got to know the interviewees. The system kept us separate but also allowed for a mutual respect to form; we have discussions instead of arguments now. While that may not be totally in line with Franzen's goals for inter-student relations, it's on the right track. If I, or all of us, had been allowed to take a course like Franzen's fourth period before, none of the early problems would have arisen or [they would have] been diminished. There's a big difference between working with someone for a week on a presentation and working with someone for the better part of three months. The cooperative skills gained from the class will undoubtedly assist us in whatever jobs we pursue after college, be it an office or research team or studio; knowing how to work with all kinds of people will come in handy.

That's the best part of the course. Editing, catering, construction, garden, or wetlands reclamation; the skills you gained are actually marketable talents. This class didn't leave us with some little credit or shard of knowledge for college, at least not in the traditional way. This class wasn't some useless filler or elective to pad out the day. This class didn't require information to be regurgitated back in assessments. This class didn't conform to a common core standard. However, it required constant, focused work and taught skills we can use anywhere. It forced us to work together and be problem solvers. It allowed me to learn about myself without sacrificing the other education. Isn't that what a class should do?

Side Note on Feasibility

Many teachers ask how we are able to do all of the things described in this book in terms of funding, permission, and safety issues. Often funding comes from our own pockets, fundraisers within the school, grants both big and small we apply for, dumpster diving, an awesome Alumni Association, local philanthropists, and probably annoying everyone we meet by talking about what we are doing in class. For permission to do all of these things, letters go out to each parent and guardian the first day of class with a massive checklist covering everything from eating student cooking to using power tools to allergy alerts. If parents know what you are up to and trust you, most of the other obstacles are just speed bumps. As far as getting administration on board, start by asking big. Each permission is a negotiation, and some just don't come out in your favor. Rely on community partners; for example, each time we build a fire, I call the fire department to give them a heads-up. The safety of students is our number one concern. In carrying out everything described in this book, the worst injury incurred has been three stitches in a thumb that got in the way of a cucumber. We design our lessons, the classroom community, and project-specific structures to ensure the safety of each student. That includes listening to students when they set boundaries. In addition, small wins at the beginning of this journey gave us increasing autonomy to push the boundaries of what a classroom can be, what students can do, and what we as teachers have the space to design. With all of that in mind, having fun is what allows these experiences to happen, be effective, and be allowed to happen again.

Stepping beyond the School Day and Classroom

Throughout this book, the idea of a "classroom" and "class time" has been a flexible concept. You might have asked, "Where did a massive garden complex come from?" "How were they able to cook a 120-person class meal?" "How did these things happen in a 42-, 56-, 72-minute period?" As well as other questions about how many of these things were occurring at once. Although I'm discussing them last, the Cooking Club and the garden were two of the first steps in creating the Food Studies program. They happened because both teachers and administration said yes at the right time to the right people without knowing where that yes would go.

Cooking Club and the garden became identities, communities, timeless spaces that existed in story, over the summer, while skipping classes, before school when you just needed to fry an egg still warm from a chicken's cloaca. Cooking

Club sometimes provided labor, whimsical ideas, invitations to another culinary world, and almost always laughter, learning, and compassion. The garden provided food, the opportunity for risk, a spot a student could own, shape, and watch grow over an extended period of time. These were institutions where students shaped the community and, through knowing they mattered, cared for and made the institution better. All of those dynamics came into our scheduled classrooms as examples and to reinforce those understandings.

These two spaces were also the hardest to manage. Cooking Club became too popular. The conflict between being inclusive to all who wanted to learn and having a strong community identity was a complication that Brent and I did not navigate successfully. The garden was super intensive in terms of time and resources, especially during the summer months when students had a tough time getting to school or small engines broke down. Both institutions could have benefited from better collaboration, communication, and more effective use of resources.

Feel free to take on these narratives for what they are: a story. Take our experiences as a warning about making conscious choices about how you design the time and spaces that are sacred to you and your students if you'd like. For me, when I re-read my own words, I see the results of the hardest I've ever worked as an educator and the potential that teaching as a soulcraft has to inspire, empower, and have impact on our students. Feel free to see it as that, too.

Cooking Club

The student who demanded that we have a cooking club showed up to the first meeting and never came back. But all of the other students he convinced to show up on the first day kept doing so. I am not a trained chef; I am a food nerd. My skills in the kitchen came from watching my mom and stepdad cook every night, grilling out every night with my college roommate Kevin, and experimenting on my own as a young twentysomething. Considering my lack of training as a chef, a decrepit home economics room filled with antique cooking utensils, old sewing machines, broken talking dolls, and an oven with only one knob seemed like a good place to start our Cooking Club.

◎   ◎   ◎   ◎

Recipe for Starting a Cooking Club
Ingredients:
Remnants of a circa 1980s home ec room
Group of inspired and passionate students
Desire to learn through food research and action

Solid speaker system

First aid kit

Aprons

Teacher who doubles as manager, grocer, safety specialist, firefighter, milk sniffer, caterer, and therapist

Procedure:

Have students vote on recipes. Run before school to get groceries. Hand kids the tools. Choose one to play tunes. Wash dishes. Sit around a table. Make hallways smell like bacon or curry or cinnamon to draw everyone in. Say thanks. Eat together. Wash more dishes.

◎　◎　◎　◎

During the school day, Room 110 housed students in Developmental English courses. Each Wednesday I would gather the groceries from my car and then start washing off the expletives written on the desks. After a couple of weeks, the teacher loaned me a few students to help me with the groceries and to wipe down the tables for the club. Out of that basic loan, I started building relationships with those students, saving wear and tear on my back, rounded up some of my favorite students and helpers, expanding the Cooking Club, and gradually noticed that there was less graffiti on the tables every morning. One of those students, Michael, became my colleague for his four years of high school. I helped him with his papers; he helped me clean dishes. I pulled him out of in-school suspension; he helped harvest in the garden. I talked to him about the struggles in his life and what I have learned about how to be a man; he became one of the pillars of Cooking Club by welcoming everyone, watching out for everyone, and defending his community with the sweat of his brow and strong words.

Cooking Club became a place where students could express themselves in a safe community while at the same time taking on a challenge that was full of risk; all you needed to do was show up and be willing to work. At the beginning of each semester, we would sit in a huge circle and brainstorm everything that we wanted to cook during those twelve weeks. The board would be covered with everything from mochi to calamari to decorated layer cakes; then we would vote. Students who won the support of their peers for their dishes came up with the recipes and ingredient lists and became kitchen managers.

The smells from 110 brought students from every social clique, academic track, sports team, and demographic of the school to the table, and we put tools in their hands. We handed eight-inch chef knives to kids who weren't allowed to have real silverware in the lunchroom. We asked students to create dishes for real audiences with taste buds and digestive tracts who would grade their work, sometimes literally and sometimes just with a high five. We questioned how if we are what we eat, what are we when we eat what is at home or in the cafeteria or from the garden or within the Cooking Club. Kids found that they were capable of a lot more than the adults around them gave them credit for. They found they could create the smells, tastes, and emotions that made a home, and the other students flocked to experience that. Each time we finished cooking, we brought it back to the circle around the table to acknowledge what we had made, how it had turned out, ways to improve, and, of course, to tip our hats to the chefs.

Soon we were packed. In addition, Cooking Club became a natural extension of the Food Lit course, encompassing current students as well as junior and senior alumni. The students who had spent months honing skills in the club started passing them down, becoming teachers in their own right. The club started taking on a life of its own; it became easier to run, and my role transformed from that of teacher to that of manager. Many of the students started rivaling my own skills as a cook, and luckily, Brent, a former chef of nine years, made Cooking Club a regular event on his schedule. We expanded, taking over the Senior Citizens Center, a former faculty lounge with a kitchen that had been claimed by a group of retired alumni as their own for bridge on most days. Accepting the occasional spittle shot out from between hastily glued dentures

Learning how to use local and seasonal ingredients of country ham and asparagus.

when my students left food scraps in their sink, moved the chair cushions, or used the senior citizens' butter was worth it to be able to take in more kids. Some of these senior citizens became our biggest supporters in the Alumni Association and in sharing their garden wisdom as we got to know each other better. It was worth the call home when a student missed a cucumber and hit a thumb. It was worth waking up at 4 a.m. to do the grocery runs on club days. It was worth using my own money in the faint hope that the school would reimburse me. It was worth it to see the students grow in confidence when they perfected a skill they could use to make someone else happy both mentally and physically, especially on days when students entered Room 110 downtrodden from being told they were failures. It was worth it to see students who thought they had nothing to give prepare a Thanksgiving meal and invite their favorite teachers. It was worth it to see Michael go from a student labeled as having a behavioral disability to a leader and now out on his own, and to see Sydnea, who led the

Teaching all-important knife skills.

cooking team to second place in the state competition, go to Sullivan culinary school. Cooking Club became the most rewarding part of my life as a teacher.

When students choose to be somewhere, it doesn't matter what their ACT scores are. That choice empowers them to work toward success. Our job is to set the bar higher. For four years running, we have catered the 150-strong alumni breakfast during fall homecoming. The students take over the cafeteria kitchen, learning how to use the "combi oven," work the serving line, work the crowd (they already are experts from daily handshakes and greetings), and welcome some old Creekers back home with a warm plate of food. Some recipes have become famous. A server from the Mayan Café, an amazing restaurant and local supporter of the Food Studies work at FCHS, tipped us onto a pumpkin bread pudding with maple syrup that was being served as a seasonal treat. We copied it, making our own adjustments and scaling it up. Not anticipating the subsequent love for the dish, I didn't make copies of the recipe, which led to a constant email conversation with alumni from across the state, as I had daily demands for the recipe in preparation for family Thanksgiving meals. That recipe allowed us to time travel and teleport as we reconnected Fern Creek High School to the current homes of alumni, enlarging our community and securing many willing donors and supporters as the program expanded.

Our students started to demand more. Some formed teams and competed at the Farm to School Junior Chef competition. Our Mama's Italian Soup took second place, was taken up by the district, prepared for the whole school, and is still demanded by faculty when winter starts to kick in. Some students wanted to give to the community, so we traveled to the Shawnee Fresh Stop Market, a biweekly neighborhood-run CSA built on a sliding scale to make fresh, good food available to people at all income levels, used the seasonal and local produce provided, and taught our recipe to the patrons as we served samples through the store's kitchen window. Some students turned providing food into a business by creating a student-run catering company designed for the needs of teachers, cooking healthy, affordable meals for the faculty each week and delivering them as those hard workers left on Friday afternoon. Some students looked inward to help, making frozen family-sized pans of lasagna for the family of one of our members whose father had died of cancer, delivering them with warm wishes of sympathy and hugs. Some students just got a meal filled with love, which, sadly for some, is hard to come by.

We have made kimchi, Bosnian pita, eight-pound dry rubbed pork butts, sushi, thousands of cookies, fresh pasta, handmade mozzarella, Nepali pyaji, bacon maple pancake cakes, samosas, numerous Thanksgiving dinners, pho, bread from scratch, old family recipes, and new ones that sometimes even taste good. Cooking Club has become a place to explore the world that we are sometimes not able to explore in the classroom or in home kitchens. Young men who are not allowed in the kitchen at home have secretly frosted cupcakes. Young women who are quiet and polite in the classroom have found strong voices when the dishwashers are snapping towels, the onions are chopped, not diced— "I said DICED, dammit!"

Room 110 has allowed teachers and students to work together in collective labor toward an end goal that usually results in sitting around a table, laughing with your mouth full, looking across the plates into the eyes of both friends and strangers. This collective weekly endeavor has created relationships that have influenced students' performance in the classroom, young adults' relationships with their families, the individual's sense of self-worth and identity, and learners' ability to see that knowledge isn't always restricted to a desk and a closed mouth but instead can involve moving with purpose, tools in hand, saliva building, for the next morsel of information to be conveyed through taste bud, fingertip, olfactory neurons, or line in a recipe.

Cooking Club Reflection (Denis D.)

I joined Cooking Club because I loved cooking, simple as that. I thought it was just going to be a club in which a group of students cooked a meal, ate it, then repeated the next week. It was far more than that. I learned how to grow and harvest my own food. I learned how to combine flavors to make something taste amazing. I learned the necessary skills to cook, skills I can actually use at home, unlike some of the subjects in school. I acquired a new way of looking at food. I started to understand the importance of eating healthy as well as how to make my favorite dishes at home healthier. The first day staying for Cooking Club I learned that I wasn't the only kid that already "knew" how to cook, and by that I mean know how to make more than just Ramen in a cup. I got to see some self-proclaimed veteran chefs, students that cook every day for their little brothers and sisters while their parents were at work. I also saw students that had never cooked before a day in their life, but were interested in learning.

I had joined Cooking Club on Brainstorm-What-We-Will-Make-For-Our-Thanksgiving- Club-Meal Day. Everything was very informal, people shouting what their families made every Thanksgiving and the dishes we just HAD to try. This was an especially unique experience for me. I was the first child in my family to be born in the United States. All of my older relatives were born in Bosnia. Sure I know what Thanksgiving is, but my family never really celebrated it. Listening to all of the other students list foods that they loved for Thanksgiving made me realize that I had never associated a food from my family with Thanksgiving, so I decided that I would make something I knew no one in that room had eaten before: Bosnian Pita.

Growing up, pita was a staple in my house. Bosnian pita is like a very thin bread filled with a variety of different things. You can make pita filled with ground beef (burek), pita filled with cottage cheese and egg (sirnica), or pita filled with spinach or other vegetables (zeljanica). I decided that this would be the dish that I made for the Thanksgiving Meal. It is pretty simple as far as ingredients go, but the process is what the others found fascinating. There is no American dish that is comparable to it, that's why it's so hard to describe.

As the year progressed, I could really see myself getting better at cooking in a variety of ways. I was no longer strictly following a recipe to reproduce a result, I was learning to combine flavors and make something that tasted good, but didn't mock a recipe. When the teacher saw how far we had come, we cooked for people other than ourselves and our families; we got to cook for people we

Denis, Irma, and the Cooking Club stretch the dough.

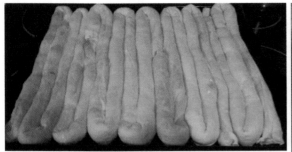

The dough is lined with beef and onions, rolled, coiled, and ready for the oven.

The most beautiful and delicious thing you will ever eat: Bosnian pita.

didn't know. Nothing I have ever done was comparable to the joy I got when we cooked downtown for people at the Redeemer Lutheran Church. It was a church used by the volunteer-run non-profit New Roots that provides bi-weekly CSA opportunities for low income families at pop-up farmers markets called Fresh Stops. We got to cook for people that didn't really get the chance to eat a home cooked meal that often, whether that be because of access to fresh foods, a broken family, late shifts, or simply because it was more time and more expensive than heading over to the the nearest fast food restaurant.

I remember seeing all different types of people enjoying the lo mein we made with the ingredients that were available to them in their CSA share, and the smiles it brought to their faces. The meal that we made could just as easily be made by them with the fresh ingredients they were getting, and we ended up making copies of the recipe that the people took home with them. I remember seeing the elementary school girl walk in and how she instantly wanted to help, so we let her. At that point, I realized that Cooking Club was a lot more important than just an afternoon snack; it had the power to provide many more people a meal, a recipe, a smile that lasts them the whole day, and can reach to more people later on. There have been no other classes or clubs that I have experienced this kind of reach to the community.

Cooking for other people made me realize how much I enjoyed to cook, and I decided that the Cooking Team was the perfect opportunity for me to reach out even farther from just a small kitchen downtown; the new target was JCPS [Jefferson County Public Schools]. The theme of the cooking competition later in the year was to make a dish that could be served in cafeterias all across JCPS. The restrictions we had on our dish mirrored the food restrictions on all JCPS foods: whole wheat, low fat, oven temperatures, etc. If we won, Fern Creek Cooking Club reaches over 100,000 people. We decided that making a pizza would be the best way to reach out to the youth because . . . well, who doesn't like pizza? Our first time making the pizza wasn't too good. As it turns out, healthy food doesn't taste the same as our typical delicious greasy pizza we are accustomed to. The wheat crust was rubbery, the white cheese sauce wasn't great, and the only thing that made it resemble a decent pizza was the chicken and spinach toppings.

That was the only time I have ever encountered such a barrier in cooking. The challenge was no longer cooking, it was making something taste good and still follow all restrictions placed by JCPS food guidelines. Then I realized that cooking restrictions are part of the lives of millions of Americans. Many people are diabetic, have food allergies, or have a dietary preference that restricts them from eating a variety of foods. Thankfully I didn't have to make a gluten-free, dairy-free, vegetarian pizza, but even still, the challenge set forth was not an easy obstacle to overcome.

Countless attempts at making a delicious and healthy pizza were made before we decided to look for a professional. Our coach, and Fern Creek alumna, Sydnea, took second place at competition the three years before. She decided it would be good for us to meet with her teachers to see if they could show us how to correct our errors. We made a trip over to Sullivan University, where we got to talk and cook with actual chefs and learn the secrets behind cooking. Not only did we learn how to prepare the pizza well, we got to share a unique experience that made me understand why I loved to cook. I loved being with people, learning their story through the food that they eat. I got to learn about the traditions of people and why they loved to cook with their families. Cooking is the simplest and easiest way to connect with people that mean the most to you in your life, and share a piece of you that you couldn't share in any conversation or class.

Again, we practiced. Now, edibility wasn't the issue, it was perfecting the pizza. A little more cheese and a little less balsamic vinaigrette. I think the best part about the whole thing was "taste-testing" each slice. Consistency is very important.

I'll never forget competition day. We all woke up pretty early in the morning and met at the school. We filled plastic tubs full of everything we would need: cutting boards, mixing bowls, measuring cups and spoons, knives, etc. We all piled into a minivan and headed off to the state fair. Being the only boy in the group, I was expected to do all of the heavy lifting, which everyone else found hilarious. I was standing up on stage when it hit me. Holy crap, I'm here. I'm going to cook for judges. They are going to judge my food. I'm going to be on TV! I felt a little overwhelmed. Then I looked at the other team also on stage. Another school that obviously had way too much money to spend on a cooking team. Each member had a dark maroon chef jacket and hat, a nametag, and what looked to be brand new cooking equipment. Here I was, standing on stage in front of a crowd of people and cameras, wearing sweatpants and a Fern Creek t-shirt. I wanted to run off that stage and never look back, but I remembered that I wasn't there for everyone else, I was there for me. I was there because I loved cooking. I was there because my friends were there. I was there because I wanted to make a difference in the food served at my school. So I stayed. And I cooked.

We lost first round. The team, as well as I, were frustrated. We were all talking bad about the other team because we worked harder for it, we made something unique, we didn't take the easy way out, but none of that really mattered. They were the exact same as us. They were part of this team because they loved to cook, same as us. Winning or losing didn't matter, it was cooking that mattered. Cooking with people that meant something to me was what mattered.

◎   ◎   ◎   ◎

Pita Recipe
Dough Ingredients:
5 C flour
"Enough" C warm water
Salt
Filling Ingredients:
1½ lb ground beef
1 onion
½ C water
Salt and pepper
Vegeta

Dough Instruction 1:
In a large mixing bowl, combine the flour, water, and salt. Form into ball and let sit for 5–10 minutes. Knead the dough again, then place on a floured plate and rub with oil. Let stand for 10–15 minutes.

Meat Instruction:
In a large bowl, combine the ground beef, diced onion, salt, pepper, and Vegeta. Once combined, add water until the meat holds its shape but is very easy to pull apart (this will help with the rolling part later on).

Dough Instruction 2:
Clear off a large table and spread a tablecloth/sheet (this will help with the rolling step).
Place dough in the center of the table, and begin to roll out the dough until it is roughly 2 or 3 feet in diameter. Rub more oil on the dough and let stand for 5–10 more minutes. Begin stretching the dough. The desired thickness is as thin as you can get it without tearing the dough. If you can almost see through the dough, you're doing good!

Filling:
Fill with the meat mixture. It is easiest to take small handfuls and flick it on the dough. You don't want large chunks because it won't cook evenly. You don't need to cover the whole thing at once. Cover roughly 4–6 inches, then roll. Cut off the roll you just made and put it in a well-oiled pan. You can swirl it into one large pita, zigzag it like I did, or do small individual servings in a little swirl. It's up to you!

Bake:
Bake at 400°F for about 35–45 minutes, or until the crust is golden brown. Let stand 5 minutes before serving.

ENJOY!

◎　◎　◎　◎

Pita has always been one of those comfort foods growing up. My mom learned how to make it from a very young age. She told me how her mother taught her how to cook it, and that it was one of those meals that you can eat any time of the day.

Bosnia isn't the richest country in the world. During time of war, money was tight, but pita still found its way to the table.

Learning how to make pita is learning about my mom's life as a child. When they made burek, they didn't really have a Walmart that they could buy from. They either had a neighbor that had a bunch of cows (in which they traded stuff for), or they had to go all the way into town to get to a butcher shop.

Cooking Club Reflection (Irma D.)

It was intimidating being a freshman because I always felt like an underdog, and not knowing anyone didn't help either. I have always had trouble making friends because I'm such a shy person. However, I decided to step out of my comfort zone one day by joining Cooking Club. All my life I had a passion for cooking and I thought it would be awesome to be in a club dedicated to it. But as soon as I stepped through the doors, I heard people laughing; I saw people working together and I realized it wasn't going to just be about cooking. It was going to be about friendship, leadership, and community. One week Mr. Franzen sat everyone down in a circle and he told us that we were going to make food from cultures around the world.

I immediately became excited because I grew up in a Bosnian household with food that is completely different than food in the United States. I thought this would be the perfect time to show everyone one of the best foods that exist: Pita.

Pita is a typical Bosnian meal that can be made many ways. You start off by making a dough and stretching it until it's almost see-through, roughly four or five feet in diameter. To stretch the dough, place your hands underneath it, palms up, and softly pull it toward you. You then fill it with whatever you like such as ground beef with onion, potatoes, cottage cheese, cabbage, etc. I decided to make the typical Pita with ground beef and onions. However, I was one of the only people who knew how to make it, yet I had five people in my group. This meant that I had to become the leader, something I've never done before. When I was showing everyone how to roll and stretch the dough, they were amazed. People from other groups would stop what they were doing and before I knew it, I had 30 pairs of eyeballs staring at me. It was frightening at first, but it really allowed me to step out of my shell. I wasn't the shy girl who didn't talk anymore, but I was the loud girl who would shout across the room to my team member to grab me a mixing bowl. Some of the people in Cooking Club would look at me astonished, thinking, "who is this girl? I've never heard her speak in class." Cooking Club allowed me to be myself, and be someone other than the quiet girl who is always on task. I was able to speak out when we were sharing ideas and contribute my thoughts in a conversation.

School was no longer classwork and homework, it was friendship, leadership, and community. I had people to walk down the hall with between classes and people would stop me and say hi. Cooking Club changed my whole high school experience because I was finally a part of something, and I was able to be myself. Because of those weekly meetings, I feel like a more outgoing person overall. I participate more in my classes and I'm not afraid to share my ideas. Overall, I feel like I have improved my social skills because of Cooking Club. People were always there pushing me to be myself and encouraging me to share my ideas. But I also noticed other people becoming more outgoing and friendly to others. When there would be a new face in Cooking Club, everyone made sure to make them feel welcomed and part of the community. We asked for their ideas and their input on whatever the project was and within a few weeks, they were becoming leaders and teaching others their skills.

FC Alumni Breakfast Recipe: Pumpkin Bread Pudding with Caramel Sauce

Bread pudding
    2 C half-and-half
    1 15-oz can pure pumpkin

1 C (packed) plus 2 Tbsp dark brown sugar
2 large eggs
1½ tsp pumpkin pie spice
1½ tsp ground cinnamon
1½ tsp vanilla extract
10 C ½-inch cubes egg bread, croissants, and/or day-old donuts (about 10 oz)
½ C golden raisins
Caramel sauce
1¼ C (packed) dark brown sugar
½ C (1 stick) unsalted butter
½ C whipping cream
Powdered sugar

Preparation

For bread pudding:
Preheat oven to 350°F. Whisk half-and-half, pumpkin, dark brown sugar, eggs, pumpkin pie spice, cinnamon, and vanilla extract in large bowl to blend. Fold in bread cubes. Stir in golden raisins. Transfer mixture to 11" × 7" glass baking dish. Let stand 15 minutes. Bake pumpkin bread pudding until tester inserted into center comes out clean, about 40 minutes.

Meanwhile, prepare caramel sauce:
Whisk brown sugar and butter in heavy medium saucepan over medium heat until butter melts. Whisk in cream and stir until sugar dissolves and sauce is smooth, about 3 minutes.

Sift powdered sugar over bread pudding. Serve warm with caramel sauce.

◎ ◎ ◎ ◎

The Garden

For me, the garden is constantly filled with students. It began as a field of grass next to the gravel parking lot. We started seven years ago by putting up a gutter, a rain barrel, and three garden beds. I bought the gutter materials, someone donated the barrel, and I scavenged the wood. When a student looked up after applying sealant to the gutter seam and said, "I love this and want to do this for my job," I knew I was onto something important. We tried to sell four paper bags of collard greens that spring but got stiffed. It was a season for learning.

We teamed up with the district to execute a massive grant from the Centers for Disease Control to fight childhood diabetes and obesity by building gardens throughout the school district. After we trained kids on the tools, they

FCHS Tigers planting a spring garden in mayonnaise buckets.

built twenty-six school gardens and each time fell asleep in the back of my Toyota Matrix that also served as our job truck. Once those gardens were completed, we turned our eyes to that blank field by the school that now featured a greenhouse surrounded by a new fence. Heavy mayonnaise (HM) buckets became our farm. The district gave us hundreds of slick, marginally washed HM buckets to fill with soil and then plants. We rocked it out and groaned whenever we grabbed a gob of old sun-ripened mayo when moving the plants. Basil was the main crop, and we sent some back to the school's central kitchen with the goal of trying to provide food for the school district.

The cedar wood arrived, and my kids got to work. Students drew blueprints using graph paper and finally had a reason to use math. The whole class handled chop saws, impact drivers, shovels, and drills, and went to the next class with cedar dust stuck to their skin with sweat. The garden beds came in all shapes—traditional rectangles, arrows, triangles, pentagons, an octagon, multileveled, and with benches built in. Soil thrown in—plants from the greenhouse—food coming out. The garden quickly went from a gutter, rain barrel, and three beds to a compound. It was already filling up with the memories of construction as the initial builders were graduating. The fruits of the students' work stayed behind with me to tell their story.

Ducks. Chickens. Fruit trees. Composting. The compound diversified, and students took on the tasks. The ducks and chickens were cared for by students who arrived at 6:30 a.m. before school; I would find them watering the beds, eating from the beds, and hugging chickens when I rolled into work at 6:35 a.m.

A student-based culture started to emerge around the garden: the ducks and chickens got names (RIP Afro-Chicken), individual tomato plants were claimed, art pieces were added to beautify the space, and students started giving tours and sharing knowledge without my permission or awareness. The work went from being Franzen's Project to The Garden.

Environmental Club poses while building passive solar chicken coop.

Students continued to build and add on, sometimes as part of class, as with the brick grill, the pavilion, and the picnic tables. The Environmental Club became the work-in-the-garden club, taking care of the plants in the greenhouse and garden beds, building a passive solar chicken coop, a recycled material chicken coop, as well as an outdoor sink. Summer workers funded by the FCHS Alumni Association maintained the garden over the summer and started selling produce, first at a farmers market, then at a school garden stand, and now they share the produce with their families, neighbors, and school personnel.

Once the fenced-in area was filled, we built up, out, and down. Birdhouses and a chicken weathervane went up in the sky. Fifty apple, pear, plum, persimmon, hazelnut, cherry, chestnut, and pawpaw trees found homes radiating out to the edge of campus. The meaning of these places grew deeper. A garden bed was named and painted in memory of a young Nepali student who passed away, and the ELL class planted an orchard of pawpaw trees in his memory that is expanded each year. Now, instead of three trees on a hillside, the memorial is a pawpaw patch in the midst of 110 trees meant to reforest the headwaters of the Lesser Fern Creek.

Working in the garden, I know I am just a steward. In that space, students have found passions, developed a love for learning, grieved while hugging chickens, shared meals, learned how to use tools, discovered what it means to build, cut themselves and bled, been trusted with dangerous things, laughed with one another, and seen the progress of their work, whether it grew green out of the ground, came together with screws, became palatable with fire, or returned to the earth through decay. I am there to keep those sacred things safe and to tell the stories that make them sacred. Each time we go there now, students know the garden is a special place. One can't help but recognize the passion, thought, and time that has made it a landscape of expressed learning and compassion.

How to Start or Resurrect a School Garden

Starting a garden can be intimidating. That said, start with the basics by assessing where you are: Can you use the soil already present? Do you need raised beds? What is your growing zone? Do you have access to water? Will you have summer help? Are fruit trees a better option? What infrastructure is already in place? What community resources are available? What is your own knowledge level? How will the garden take your teaching somewhere you haven't been?

Gardens can look like five-gallon buckets with holes drilled in the bottom, a square of reclaimed lumber defining an area of tilled soil, or multiple in-ground beds. All of these start with saying yes and putting a shovel in some soil. Ask administrative permission and start small. Make sure your passions and time capacity match the obligation and responsibility. If you take on too much and fail, you might lose the good faith that allowed the start. Grow easy wins: basil can be propagated through cuttings, cherry tomatoes produce many small fruits that allow you to share the experience, strawberries can be ready at the end of the school year, loose leaf lettuce can be grown quickly and become a class salad with tons of variations.

If you already have infrastructure in place at your school, get students excited about planning a garden resurrection party. Get someone, ideally parents or administration, to volunteer their grill and put out the word. Have an organized to-do list for partygoers so that when people show up, in addition to eating they have work to do, feel accomplished, and experience a productivity that will link them to the space and have them coming back. Reach out to your Agricultural Extension Service, local Master Gardener Program, senior citizens (a massive underutilized community resource), and parents. Ask hardware stores, small and big, and seed catalog businesses for donations. Once seed is a year old, they can't legally sell it; we would get boxes every year with 90-percent-plus germination rates. I've been amazed at the support we've had from strangers and organizations once people began talking in their social networks.

Take the time to help students develop patience. Have comfortable seats around the garden or next to your bucket. Understand that sitting in a garden quietly and thinking is now rare for our kids and is actually progress, an ability to detach from the siren call of 24/7 technology. Make sure you keep yourself grounded to the garden with reminders of how having dirt under your fingernails has shaped you; those experiences are what students will see, hear, and feel as genuine and keep them coming back.

Questions to Chew On

1. What are the green spaces around your school?

2. Who would be your allies in starting a garden at your school?

3. What would be your goal in taking a class to work in a garden or natural area?

4. Gardening self-awareness is important: What color is your thumb?

(Don't worry, teachers can learn, too.)

We Built It (Matthew W.)

I was a student that, for the majority of my school career, woke up, went to school and rode home. I played games or reluctantly did homework and started over again every day. Until my freshman year, a teacher hosted a canoe field trip for the students that had done well in his class. I was one of those students, and that was the first canoeing trip I had ever been on. I enjoyed being outside away from school and everything else. That one canoe trip was what I feel partially led me later on to wanting to join Environmental Club.

Where I ended up going, on the wrong day but in the same place, was Cooking Club. Not what I wanted to do, Cooking Club, but the busses had left and I wouldn't have a way home till after it was over—so, I stayed. I don't remember what we made that

FCHS class of 2013, former garden manager, future mechanical engineer graduating from University of Louisville's Speed School of Engineering. Matthew took every one of the Food Studies courses except Food Lit. However, he became a regular co-teacher in Food Lit as an upperclassman and alumnus. He's a key example of how students are drawn to constructive community while at the same time build it through peer-to-peer teaching, authentic engagement, and ownership of the community as a physical place and as a social web.

day. However, I enjoyed taking basic ingredients that on their own are nothing spectacular, but when put together with some love and care created a beautiful dish. Week after week in Cooking Club, that's exactly what we did, take boring mundane items and make them delicious. That led me to become passionate about this new-found skill. A skill and a passion that would lead me to be involved with catering the alumni breakfast while a student and even as an alumni myself. I also ended up being a member of Fern Creek's Italian Stallions cooking team as a fill in after another member realized they couldn't continue with it through the summer. I stepped up and spent the following months practicing the dish with Sydnea Johnson and Austin Kettwig in the first Kentucky

Farm to School Junior Chefs competition. We placed second, in the competition, with a modified recipe of grandmother Kettwig's famous soup (all grandmothers have a famous dish). Something I'm quite proud of considering that I hadn't really cooked much at all prior to joining Cooking Club. Furthermore, most of the ingredients we used in the soup were seeded and cared for by myself and the rest of Environmental Club that summer. In addition, this recipe was served in the cafeteria the following school year to the entire school.

Recipe: Mama's Italian Soup

1½ lb ground Italian sausage
2 white onions
5 carrots
1 bulb garlic
5 stalks celery
1 qt chicken stock
3 lbs red potatoes
2 qt water
½ bunch kale
2 sprigs rosemary
Salt, pepper to taste
Parsley (decoration)

Dice all veggies into bite-size pieces. Place potatoes in an oven-safe pan at 350° F for 45 minutes. Brown the sausage. Sauté sausage, onions, carrots, celery, and garlic 10–15 minutes on medium heat. Add water and chicken stock to the veggies. Add sprigs of rosemary. When potatoes are done, add them to the pot and cook an additional 10 minutes. Remove sprigs of rosemary. Add in kale and allow to cook for 5 minutes. Salt and pepper to taste.

Though Cooking Club was great and I'm glad that I stayed and went on to do the things I did, what I really wanted at the time was to go to Environmental Club. On my first day of Environmental Club we planted trees. Simple enough, right? Except about halfway through my vision started to go white, and I dropped to my knees in order to keep from passing out. This was something I had experienced before, and knew I needed to cool off and drink some water. I was disappointed with myself, feeling that I had failed in some way. I went back the next week and the next, getting more involved with each meeting. Soon we started to make the first of what would be many attempts at an outdoor classroom. That is where I used my first power tool to mount the white board on its posts. With my involvement, I started to value physical labor more whether it be weeding or driving fencing stakes into the ground. It was very good at clearing my mind, allowing me to take a step back and re-approach something I had hit a roadblock on from a different view. Manual labor, I also found, makes talking easier; I don't know if it's the shared common goal or what, but when working I find it easier to talk.

Watching the school gardens grow from a few mayonnaise buckets with herbs in them to the current compound with a greenhouse, power and water, tools, an orchard with now fruit bearing trees, and chickens is impressive and kind of hard to believe that so much of it happened in the couple of years after I initially joined Environmental Club. A massive change in the course of a few years, all built off the effort [of] Franzen, Peters, other students, and myself. For me, the gardens are more than the soil, boards, and screws that built the area; it is the stories and memories of people and things we did.

For example, when the first baby chicks arrived in the mail before we started hatching our own, we built an enclosure for them. We were proud of our work; that is until the day when something got in and killed 6 of our baby chicks. We collectively spent the day armoring their enclosure with chicken wire so that no more could be harmed. Then there was the time Quentin, Spencer, and I spent a few hours one weekend building and troubleshooting a ballista out of scrap wood, a few bolts, and a bicycle inner tube. In retrospect, it was something we probably shouldn't have made at school. Of course, it was dismantled before anything nefarious could happen.

In many ways, I feel my experiences in the garden with the plants and animals brought me closer to my grandfather who for many years was a farmer and machinist. I know he loved me, but I always kind of felt like he saw me as a city kid that couldn't do much. After getting excited about growing food and caring for chickens and ducks we seemed to have more to talk about, and I started to know him better. It also helped that I started using power tools and wanting to make things. I pulled scrap wood boards and a tar paper roll out of the dumpster from a roof repair, and brought home broken toasters and other junk. Seeing every scrap of wood and metal, just as my grandfather did, as something that could be turned into something new giving life to something discarded. This mentality—that almost everything can be repurposed—was probably reinforced by the chicken coops and everything else that we built was made from discarded wood and pallets.

By the end of senior year, I spent most mornings before classes restocking the chicken's food and water and just chillin' in their area before heading in the building. During the day, I would do my normal class work but sometimes in math class, if I had finished my work ahead of time, I would ask to go work in the garden. Often it was yes, others no, but, when I was able, I went out and watered plants, weeded. General maintenance around the place, even pulling weeds out of the dirt, is better than sitting in class waiting for something else to happen or the class to end.

From that effort, I was offered the chance to be the Alumni Farm Manager. In a way, the garden went from just friends working together to where I had some responsibility to make sure my friends did what they needed so that we could keep things running smoothly and without issue. This role, to be honest, wasn't all that smooth the first summer. There was a lot of letting some of the more mundane things like weeding slide for a bit, then realizing we really needed to whip things back into shape. I'd like to think I did get better at keeping on top of things. But something I feel that last summer I worked regularly tried to teach me is that you can't always solve a problem by yourself and sometimes you just need to call someone else for help, wisdom or support.

An example of this was in the months/weeks before the summer started. Franzen was looking for people that had worked hard and [that he] thought he could trust to work and be respectful to fill summer garden intern positions. Myself and a few others had vouched for one student despite some questionable beliefs he held, as he had been working very hard helping the garden move forward with new projects. Unfortunately, pretty much as soon [as] the summer started he disappeared, and no one had seen him at the gardens. I tried to contact him to see what was up but got nothing. After a couple days of failed contact I called Franzen to see if he could figure things out and as far as I know it was dealt with. What was up or how things went I don't know, but it definitely wasn't something I could have taken care of by myself.

Just as I expanded my social toolbox, I have sought many other tools and have slowly, over time, been building my own workshop. As a start of that workshop I did research into metal working and knew I couldn't afford a welder to try and learn, so I looked for something a little more manageable and fell upon aluminum, as its readily available in the form of cans and other scrap and more importantly it melts at a sweltering 660.3 Celsius (1,221°F) which is easily achievable with some charcoal and a blower. FYI—it's way simpler than it sounds. I got some garden pavers as cheap bricks to contain the charcoal, used an empty propane cylinder to hold my crushed soda cans, and used my mom's hair dryer to force air past the coals (not the happiest she's probably been but it wasn't damaged), and some long metal tongs to pull the can out of the fire so I could pour the now molten aluminum into a muffin tin to get conical frustum ingots. My intent with this project is to eventually move into sand casting.

I am currently two semesters away from having my Bachelor's Degree in Mechanical Engineering from the University of Louisville while working in product development/quality control for Sunstrand, a bio-materials company bringing sustainable natural fibers as an alternative to plastic and glass fibers as they are biodegradable, less dense, aiding in weight reduction for composite parts, and in many cases replacing synthetic fibers with natural fibers[, which] results in overall cost reduction. Additionally the hurd/shive (woody core of the hemp/kenaf/flax) material is currently sold in bulk supplies to customers who have their own uses for the particulate, but is mainly sold as a high aspect ratio filler material. Due to the responsibilities at my new job, I have not been able to devote as much time to the [FCHS] garden or kitchen as I would like. Nonetheless, I am grateful for the experience and all that it has done for me.

Did I turn either of these interests, cooking and gardening, into my career? Not directly. However, working in the garden led to me using power tools for the first time. I learned the basics of growing crops. This led me to connecting to my grandfather on a new level. I was able to make friends and awaken my curiosity about food and tools. My experiences with Fern Creek Environmental and Cooking Clubs did not put me on a straight path to my career; however, the scenic route was a lot more fun. I am forever grateful for the opportunities offered me and look forward to the day when I can become the Franzen to another Whaley.

Pulling It Together

High school is weird in that every four years the majority of a community leaves. During those fours years, the individual goes through massive changes as they mature and figure out who they are. Too often these are years to struggle through and, hopefully, forget. What the Food Studies program has been able to do is blur the lines between home and school, individual and community, learning and fun, disciplines and reality. Through that process, which allows space and time for students to engage inside and outside of class on their own terms, we often see students own their identity, the space around them, and their community. That ownership translates into responsibility and empowerment. I know this because students text me about something that reminded them of their time in high school, or I see them continuing a passion they pursued in the program. Instagram and Facebook accounts related to the program highlight how students are continuing to design and create spaces that represent their needs and desires.

What I have realized is that the collaborative work between Brent, myself, the students, and so many school and community partners transcends the pitfalls of many innovative high school programs that fail when a charismatic teacher leaves, the founding group of students graduates, or an initial grant expires. The set of Food Studies norms and culture gets passed down as students cycle out, so all around the new kids are the standards of project- and community-based multidisciplinary learning and action in physical form when they see the artifacts from past Panzenlands, forty-plus raised garden beds, alumni who take time to come back and teach, the ten-foot bald cypress trees that filter Fern Creek, grapes for eating when they get off the bus, and strawberries when they graduate.

The most challenging element to pass down are the stories as students move on. I'm not sure whether anyone besides Brent and I know that it was originally Edwin, a senior working in Environmental Club and on a nascent long-term project, who wrote the grant to plant the first apple trees in the orchard. Although names are carved on the student-constructed pavillion, do those eating under it know that the pillars came from a cherry tree that blew over on campus and that a local volunteer group helped us harvest and pour the footings for it? How do I know that some of these meaningful stories have been lost? The pipes in the greenhouse froze and exploded *again* this year; and Amanda, the school physical manager, and I walked into a frozen fountain of water at the same place that water froze six years ago. Keeping stories alive would have saved Mr. Hamilton, the building supervisor, some work.

We hope that *Say Yes to Pears* preserves some of the stories that define the Food Studies program at Fern Creek High School and that have shaped the years and characters of the students who have made the program what it is. In addition, we hope that these stories encourage and facilitate you to say yes to pears or your passions or whatever serendipitous opportunity presents itself, but also that you say yes to all that will lead to for your classroom, your school, your students, and you. Even though saying that first yes might seem intimidating and following in the footsteps of a large program like Food Studies might seem daunting, everything we have done and accomplished started with some adults and some students taking that first step without knowing what would come next.

Questions to Chew On

1. What are the characteristics of the enduring culture at your school?

2. What are the stories being preserved and which seem to have been forgotten or ignored?

3. How are you preserving the good work in your class to model as a standard for the next group of students?

4. What are the actions, ideas, and passions you need to give yourself permission to say yes to?

Afterword

Joe Franzen

We submitted the first manuscript of this book, at the time titled *Tigers Feeding Chickens*, in the spring of 2017. Since then I have left Fern Creek High School and Kentucky, moving to Olean, New York, and started teaching at Cuba-Rushford School District, a rural system with a graduating class of seventy-five students max. From what I have heard and seen in pictures, the community that formed the Food Studies program has sustained and enlarged its footprint. Brent continues to manage Food Lit and expand its role in the school and through its relationship with the Bread Loaf Teacher Network. The garden has been taken over by two teachers who brought an expertise and community network that has integrated the site into the larger school garden system of Louisville. As a whole, I am relieved and proud of how the community of Food Studies has continued.

Each time we spoke at the NCTE Annual Convention and to other teachers outside of our community, they always focused on the obstacles to a program like ours, such as meeting standards, convincing administration, funding, lack of autonomy, having time and permission to set up a program that comprised a garden, cooking, holding class meals, throwing spears, planting trees, traveling, etc. This year I found myself in a new community taking the position of teacher with a more strictly standards-regimented course, ninth-grade Global History. I no longer had the community network I once looked to for resources or the reputation to lean on when asking for permission from the powers that be to try new things. With those dynamics and the pressures of teaching a new class, I gained a greater understanding of what those teachers were concerned about, despite Cuba-Rushford being incredibly supportive of innovation and teacher collaboration.

In October I became the first implementer of the book now known as *Say Yes to Pears*. I reread the first 315-page manuscript and marked the strategies and lessons that would fit in my new teaching reality. Some were easy: handshakes, class tea, and cultural lens. Some I could adapt. The hunter-gatherer spear throwing and bison stew became Paleo-Eats, where students brought in wild meats they had hunted (squirrel, goose, venison, bear, and some local bison I bought), which I cooked in the back of the room as they wrote about the shift from the Stone Age to the Information Age. We made bread as a class while studying the Neolithic Revolution and shared loaves, replacing the pancake breakfast. We tried to cook for each unit, and I had students help with the prep before and after school: curried lentils for the Silk Road lesson, posole while learning about pre-Columbian Mesoamerican civilizations, and sniffing spices in between. Some teachers and I are also talking about writing a grant to build some high tunnels and have students bring in cuttings from the apple trees on their farms to graft a heritage-community-school orchard. The help this book gave me as I redesigned myself as a teacher in a new community convinced me that this book has meaning and value large enough to survive a title change, tough feedback, and manuscript reorganization. Writing the book was worth it because I know that it has helped at least one teacher—me. *Say Yes to Pears* made my first year in a new school an awesome one for both me and my students, who enjoyed learning, had voice, ate history, and had a safe ear to listen to them.

Thank You—Brent Peters

When I met Joe many years ago, I didn't know how important it would be to write this book. I knew when we started teaching together that our kids were seeing something new and meaningful. We were, too. I knew we had a story worth sharing. I knew we could no longer tell the story on our own. We have been to many conferences to present with our kids, and each time we have felt both exhilarated by the reception teachers have given us and disappointed at our inability to tell the full story and answer all the questions in a conference session. *Say Yes to Pears* has been our attempt to be patient with our own story and to allow it to unfold at its own pace. I will also need to read this book to remind myself of what is available so long as we say yes to the vision of teaching and learning that we know is possible.

As I think about Joe moving on now to start a new chapter in New York, I think about how as teachers part of our legacy resides in all the young people and all the fellow teachers we have the opportunity to know, work with, challenge, and see grow—and how all this gives back to us on a daily basis. Once we know a better way, we can do more with what we know. The best part of this transaction is that when we start to see and embrace what we are capable of, we

Joe and Brent on a walk in Boston in front of Harvard University, after presenting at the 2013 NCTE Annual Convention in Boston.

can really start to give back to others. This book has been our way of sharing our story and a meal with you.

Thank you for saying yes to pears and saying yes to all the possibilities in you!

Works Cited

Arno, C. Anneta, and Peter Rock. "Louisville Metro Health Equity Report." *Louisville Metro Health Equity Report 2014*, Center for Health Equity, 2014, louisvilleky.gov/sites/default/files/health_and_wellness/che/health_equity_report/her2014_7_31

Atwell, Nancie. *Lessons That Change Writers.* Heinemann, 2002.

Barber, Dan. *The Third Plate: Field Notes on the Future of Food.* Penguin, 2014.

Berry, Wendell. *Bringing It to the Table: On Farming and Food.* Counterpoint, 2009.

Burke, Jim. *What's the Big Idea? Question-Driven Units to Motivate Reading, Writing, and Thinking.* Heinemann, 2010.

Cisneros, Sandra. *Woman Hollering Creek, and Other Stories.* Random House, 1991.

Civitello, Linda. *Cuisine and Culture: A History of Food and People.* 3rd ed., Wiley, 2011.

Freire, Paulo. *Pedagogy of the Oppressed.* Continuum, 1993.

Harris, Jessica B. *High on the Hog: A Culinary Journey from Africa to America.* St. Martin's Press, 2013.

Holtz, Déborah, and Juan Carlos Mena. *Tacopedia: The Taco Encyclopedia.* Phaidon Press, 2016.

"Home Page." *Dare to Care.* daretocare.org/.

hooks, bell. *Teaching Critical Thinking: Practical Wisdom.* Routledge, 2010.

Jackson, Wes. *Consulting the Genius of the Place: An Ecological Approach to a New Agriculture.* Counterpoint, 2011.

Jurafsky, Dan. *The Language of Food: A Linguist Reads the Menu.* W. W. Norton, 2014.

Katzen, Mollie. *The Moosewood Cookbook.* New rev. ed., Ten Speed Press, 1992.

Kirkland, David. "Standpoints: Research and Teaching English in the Digital Dimension." *Research in the Teaching of English,* vol. 44, no. 1 (2009), pp.8–22.

Laidman, Jenni. "Fat City." *Louisville Magazine*, Jan. 2012.

Landay, Eileen, and Kurt Wooten. *A Reason to Read: Linking Literacy and the Arts.* Harvard Education Press, 2012.

Louv, Richard. *Last Child in the Woods: Saving Our Children from Nature-Deficit Disorder*. Algonquin Books of Chapel Hill, 2005.

Lunsford, Andrea, John J. Ruszkiewicz, and Keith Walters. *Everything's an Argument: With Readings*. 6th ed. Bedford/St. Martin's, 2012.

McCann, Colum. "Dessert." *New Yorker Online*, 12 Sept. 2011, https://www.newyorker.com/magazine/2011/09/12/dessert-colum-mccann. Accessed 27 May 2017.

McKibben, Bill. *The End of Nature*. Random House, 2006.

Nestle, Marion. *What to Eat*. North Point Press, 2006.

Newkirk, Thomas. *Minds Made for Stories: How We Really Read and Write Informational and Persuasive Texts*. Heinemann, 2014.

O'Connor, Flannery. *Mystery and Manners: Occasional Prose*. Farrar, Straus and Giroux, 1970.

Oseland, James, ed. *A Fork in the Road: Tales of Food, Pleasure, and Discovery on the Road*. Lonely Planet, 2013.

Ottolenghi, Yotam, and Sami Tamimi. *Jerusalem: A Cookbook*. Ten Speed Press, 2012.

Pant, Pushpesh, and Huma Mohsin. *Food Path: Cuisine Along the Grand Trunk Road from Kabul to Kolkata*. Roli Books, 2005.

Plato. *Republic*. Translated by C. J. Rowe, Penguin, 2012.

Pollan, Michael. *The Omnivore's Dilemma: A Natural History of Four Meals*. Penguin Books, 2006.

Postman, Neil, and Charles Weingartner. *Teaching as a Subversive Activity*. Penguin Books, 1972.

Rogers, Judy. *The Zuni Cafe Cookbook: A Compendium of Recipes and Cooking Lessons from San Francisco's Beloved Restaurant*. W. W. Norton, 2002.

Roppolo, Kimberly. "Symbolic Racism, History, and Reality: The Real Problem with Indian Mascots." *Genocide of the Mind: New Native American Writing*, edited by MariJo Moore, Thunder's Mouth Press/Nation Books, 2003, pp. 187–98.

Samuelsson, Marcus. "Face to Face with Fugu." *A Fork in the Road: Tales of Food, Pleasure, and Discovery on the Road*, edited by James Oseland. Lonely Planet, 2013, pp. 140–46.

Sinclair, Upton. *The Jungle*. Grosset and Dunlap, 1906.

Sobel, David. *Childhood and Nature: Design Principles for Educators*. Stenhouse, 2008.

———. *Place-Based Education: Connecting Classrooms and Communities*. Orion, 2013.

Spolin, Viola. *Improvisation for the Theater: A Handbook of Teaching and Directing Techniques*. 3rd ed. Northwestern UP, 1999.

Standage, Tom. *An Edible History of Humanity*. Bloomsbury, 2010.

Wallace, David Foster. *This Is Water: Some Thoughts, Delivered on a Significant Occasion about Living a Compassionate Life*. Little, Brown, 2009.

Waters, Alice. *The Art of Simple Food: Notes, Lessons, and Recipes from a Delicious Revolution.* Random House, 2007.

Wessels, Tom. *Reading the Forested Landscape: A Natural History of New England.* Countryman Press, 1999.

Young, Kevin, ed. *The Hungry Ear: Poems of Food and Drink.* Bloomsbury, 2012.

Zinn, Howard. *A People's History of the United States.* Harper, 2017.

Index

Authors

Joseph Franzen is an educator at Cuba-Rushford High School in Cuba, New York. After graduating from Washington and Lee University in Virginia, he spent eleven years in Louisville teaching, running summer programs, and working in the community. Originally from Lederach, Pennsylvania, he has brought his experience from the farm, construction crew, woods, and urban homestead into the classroom to help question traditional education and design interdisciplinary curricula. From 2010 to 2017, Franzen developed a Food Studies program with Brent Peters and a community of supporters at Fern Creek High School in Louisville, Kentucky. During that time, he earned his MAT and MeD at the University of Louisville. He lives with his wife, Elizabeth, and two daughters in Olean, New York.

Brent Peters is proud to be a teacher at Fern Creek High School in Louisville, Kentucky, where he collaborated and co-taught with Joe Franzen. He is a graduate of Bellarmine University and Middlebury College Bread Loaf School of English, and he has been teaching English and Food Lit since 2006. Before teaching, he worked as a sous-chef. Peters was Kentucky English Teacher of the Year in 2015 and the recipient of an NCTE Teacher of Excellence Award in 2015 and a Hilliard Lyons Teacher of Excellence Award in 2018. He lives in Louisville with his wife, Emily, and their two children.

This book was typeset in TheMix and Palatino by Barbara Frazier.

Typefaces used on the cover include Chronicle Display and Galaxie Polaris.

The book was printed on 60-lb. White Offset paper by Versa Press, Inc.